COLLECTION OF MASSES
OF THE
BLESSED VIRGIN MARY

Volume 2
Lectionary

COLLECTION OF MASSES OF THE BLESSED VIRGIN MARY

Volume 2

LECTIONARY

**APPROVED FOR USE IN THE
DIOCESES OF THE UNITED STATES OF AMERICA
BY THE NATIONAL CONFERENCE OF CATHOLIC BISHOPS
AND CONFIRMED BY THE APOSTOLIC SEE**

Prepared by
International Commission on English in the Liturgy
A Joint Commission of Catholic Bishops' Conferences
Washington, D.C.
and the
Secretariat for the Liturgy
National Conference of Catholic Bishops
Washington, D.C.

for Lectionary

CATHOLIC BOOK PUBLISHING CORP.
New York
1992

Concordat cum originali:
    Ronald F. Krisman, Executive Director
    Secretariat for the Liturgy
    National Conference of Catholic Bishops

Published by authority of the Committee on the Liturgy, National Conference of Catholic Bishops

ACKNOWLEDGMENTS

The English translation of the decree, introduction, psalm responses, alleluia and gospel verses, and titles and summaries of the readings from the *Lectionary for Masses of the Blessed Virgin Mary*, © 1989, 1987, International Committee on English in the Liturgy, Inc. (ICEL); excerpts from the English translation of the *Lectionary for Mass* (second edition) © 1981, 1969, ICEL; excerpts from the English translation of *Documents on the Liturgy, 1963-1975: Conciliar, Papal, and Curial Texts* © 1982, ICEL. All rights reserved.

Scripture texts used in this work are taken from the *New American Bible* Copyright © 1991, 1986, 1970 by the Confraternity of Christian Doctrine, Washington, D.C., and are used by license of the copyright owner. All rights reserved.

Arrangement of the edition, incipits, sense line and poetic line breaks, placement of headings and titles © 1991, United States Catholic Conference, 3211 4th Street, N.E., Washington, DC 20017. All rights reserved.

No portion of this work, *Lectionary for Masses of the Blessed Virgin Mary*, may be reproduced or transmitted in any form or by any means, electronic or mechanical, including photocopying, recording, or by any information storage and retrieval system, without permission in writing from the copyright owners.

T-27

NATIONAL CONFERENCE OF CATHOLIC BISHOPS
UNITED STATES OF AMERICA

In accord with the norms established by the decree of the Sacred Congregation of Rites in *Cum, nostra aetate* (27 January 1966), this edition of the *Collection of Masses of the Blessed Virgin Mary* is declared to be the vernacular typical edition of *Collectio Missarum de Beata Maria Virgine* in the dioceses of the United States of America, and is published by authority of the National Conference of Catholic Bishops.

The *Collection of Masses of the Blessed Virgin Mary* was canonically approved for use *ad interim* by the Administrative Committee of the National Conference of Catholic Bishops on 27 September 1989 and was subsequently confirmed by the Apostolic See by decree of the Congregation for Divine Worship on 20 March 1990 (Prot. N. 778/89).

As of 8 September 1992 the *Collection of Masses of the Blessed Virgin Mary* may be published and used in the liturgy. The solemnity of the Immaculate Conception, 8 December 1992, is hereby established as the effective date for the use of the *Collection of Masses of the Blessed Virgin Mary* in the dioceses of the United States of America. From that day forward no other English version may be used.

Given at the General Secretariat of the National Conference of Catholic Bishops, Washington, DC, on 31 May 1992, the feast of the Visitation.

✠ Daniel E. Pilarczyk
Archbishop of Cincinnati
President
National Conference of Catholic Bishops

Robert N. Lynch
General Secretary

CONGREGATION FOR DIVINE WORSHIP AND THE DISCIPLINE OF THE SACRAMENTS

Prot. N. 778/89

DECREE

At the request of His Excellency, the Most Reverend Daniel E. Pilarczyk, Archbishop of Cincinnati and President of the National Conference of Catholic Bishops, in a letter dated November 28, 1989, and by virtue of the faculties granted to this Congregation by the Supreme Pontiff, Pope John Paul II, we gladly approve, that is, confirm *ad interim*, the English text of the book *Collectio Missarum de Beata Maria Virgine* (Green Book), as it appears in the attached copy.

This decree, by which the requested confirmation is granted by the Apostolic See, is to be included in its entirety in the published text. Two copies of the printed text should be sent to this Congregation.

All things to the contrary notwithstanding.

From the Congregation for Divine Worship and the Discipline of the Sacraments, 20 March 1990.

✠ Eduardo Cardinal Martinez
Prefect

✠ Lajos Kada
Titular Archbishop of Tibica
Secretary

CONTENTS

8   CONTENTS

FOREWORD

Throughout its history the Church has shown a special love and devotion to Mary. The Council of Ephesus bestowed upon the blessed Virgin her highest and most significant title, Theotokos—Bearer of God, that is, Mother of God. Century after century Mary has been praised as being "higher than the cherubim and more glorious than the seraphim" because she said yes to God and through her the Word became flesh and lived among us.

As the Church has reflected on the person and life of Mary, it has come to a deeper realization of what it is to follow Christ. In fact, the early Church saw her as the model—the ideal Christian—who faithfully follows the Lord in word and action. The Second Vatican Council referred to her as the Mother of the Church, since her cooperation in God's plan for the salvation of all helped to make the existence of the Church a reality in this world.

Filled with the Holy Spirit, Mary cried out with joy that "From this day all generations will call me blessed: the Almighty has done great things for me, and holy is his Name." Mary's prophecy has become reality as the Church in the East and the West has glorified God for the humble virgin whom God has exalted for her ever-faithful love.

This collection of Masses in honor of the blessed Virgin Mary is a witness to the many ways and reasons Christians have honored Mary. These Masses are a meditation on the history of our salvation in Christ and the very nature of the Christian life. Through the use of this resource of Scripture, prayer, and praise may we join Mary in proclaiming the greatness of the Lord and ever rejoicing in God our Savior.

✠ Wilton D. Gregory
Auxiliary Bishop of Chicago
Chairman, Committee on the Liturgy
National Conference of Catholic Bishops

CONGREGATION FOR DIVINE WORSHIP

Prot. no. 309/86

DECREE

In celebrating the mystery of Christ, the Church also frequently and with deep reverence honors the Blessed Virgin Mary, because of her close bonds with her Son. She is revered by the Church as the new Eve, who, in view of the death of her Son, received at the moment of her conception a higher form of redemption. She is revered as mother, who through the power of the Holy Spirit gave virginal birth to her Son. She is revered as the disciple of Christ, who treasured in her heart the words of Christ the Master. She is revered as the faithful companion of the Redeemer, who, as God had planned, devoted herself with selfless generosity to her Son's mission.

The Church also sees in the Blessed Virgin a preeminent and unique member, graced with all virtue. The Church lovingly cherishes her and never ceases to ask for her protection, for she is the mother entrusted to us by Christ on the altar of the cross. The Church proclaims Mary as companion and sister in the journey of faith and in the adversities of life. In Mary, enthroned at Christ's side in the kingdom of heaven, the Church joyfully contemplates the image of its own future glory.

The Fathers of the Second Vatican Ecumenical Council thoroughly reviewed the Church's teaching on the place of the Blessed Virgin Mary within the mystery of Christ and his Church, and also issued principles and norms for the reform of the liturgy. As a consequence, the particular Churches as well as a number of religious institutes have composed new Mass propers. These Masses have been created on the basis of the study of ancient liturgical sources and of the writings of the Fathers of the Church of both the East and the West, on an examination of the documents of the Church's magisterium, and on a judicious balancing of the old and the new. As a result of this work of reform, existing Masses of the Blessed Virgin Mary have been accurately revised and corrected and new Masses composed.

Because of the great number of requests from pastors and the faithful and especially from rectors of Marian shrines, it seemed opportune to publish a collection selected from existing Marian Mass formularies, many of which are outstanding for their teaching, piety, and the significance of their texts. The collection was arranged to cover the cycle of the liturgical year, so that this new organ of the liturgy might foster both in communities and in individuals a genuine devotion toward the Mother of the Lord.

11

By his apostolic authority Pope John Paul II has approved the *Collectio Missarum de beata Maria Virgine* and has ordered its publication.

Therefore, by special mandate of the Pope, this Congregation for Divine Worship publishes the *Collectio Missarum de beata Maria Virgine.* The Latin text may be used as soon as the book appears. After the Holy See has reviewed the vernacular version, its use will be authorized on the date determined by the conference of bishops.

All things to the contrary notwithstanding.

From the office of the Congregation for Divine Worship, 15 August 1986, solemnity of the Assumption of the Blessed Virgin Mary.

✠ Augustin Cardinal Mayer,
Prefect

✠ Virgilio Noè
Archbishop of Voncara
Secretary

INTRODUCTION

1 In the General Introduction of the *Lectionary for Mass* there are many points on the importance of the word of God in the celebration of the eucharist that deserve careful attention.[1] Obviously all such points must be taken into careful consideration in the celebration of Masses of the Blessed Virgin Mary.

I. THE WORD OF GOD IN THE FORMULARIES OF THE *COLLECTION OF MASSES OF THE BLESSED VIRGIN MARY*

2 The particular objective of every liturgical memorial is expressed and defined through both its euchological texts and its biblical readings. It is therefore clear why even from the earliest times the greatest care has been taken in the choosing of passages of Scripture. It is also clear why each formulary in the *Collection of Masses* has been assigned its own plan of readings for the celebration of the word of God.

3 The biblical readings of the *Collection of Masses of the Blessed Virgin Mary* constitute a rich and varied corpus that in the course of the centuries has been created by the ecclesial communities of both the past and the present.

Within this biblical corpus it is possible to distinguish three types of readings:

a. readings from both the Old and the New Testament that relate to the life or mission of the Blessed Virgin or that contain prophecies about her;

b. readings from the Old Testament that from antiquity have been referred to Mary. The Fathers of the Church have always regarded the sacred Scriptures of both the Old and the New Covenant as a single corpus that is permeated by the mystery of Christ.[2] Accordingly, certain events, figures, or symbols of the Old Testament foretell or suggest in a wonderful manner the life and mission of the Blessed Virgin Mary, the glorious daughter of Zion and the mother of Christ;

c. readings of the New Testament that, while not referring to the Blessed Virgin, still are assigned to the celebration of her memorial, in order to make clear that all the virtues extolled in the Gospel—faith, charity, hope, humility, mercy, purity of heart—flourished in Mary, the first and most perfect of Christ's disciples.

4 The following points are to be noted with regard to the readings assigned to each formulary in the *Collection of Masses.*

a. Only two readings are provided; the first is from the Old Testament, from an apostle (that is, from the epistles or from Revelation) or, in the Easter season, from Acts or Revelation; the second reading is from one of the gospels. But because there are often many facets to the mystery being celebrated, frequently two or three texts are provided for the first reading and the gospel reading, one of which in each case may be chosen at will. For certain Masses, as well, two complete sets of readings are provided (see Masses 8, 31, and 39).

---

[1] See *Lectionary for Mass* (2nd *editio typica,* 1981), General Introduction, nos. 1-10.
[2] See St. Gaudentius of Brescia, *Tractatus II in Exodum,* 15: CSEL 68, pp. 26-27.

b. In special, more solemn celebrations when the priest and the faithful wish to have three readings proclaimed at Mass, the additional reading is taken from the texts provided in the *Lectionary for Mass,* the Common of the Blessed Virgin Mary, or from the texts contained in the appendix of the Lectionary of the *Collection of Masses.* The provisions of the *Lectionary for Mass,* General Introduction, section 3, nos. 78-81 ("Principles to Be Followed in the Use of the Order of Readings")* are to be observed.

c. The readings that are indicated in the *Collection of Masses* for each Mass formulary will be most appropriate for the celebration of some special memorial of the Blessed Virgin. Still, celebrants have the option of replacing these readings with other appropriate readings taken at will from those contained in the *Lectionary for Mass,* Common of the Blessed Virgin Mary, or in the appendix of the Lectionary for the *Collection of Masses.*[3]

5   The following are to be observed with regard to the liturgy of the word.

a. During the seasons of Advent, Christmas, Lent, and Easter, the readings are to be those assigned in the seasonal *Lectionary for Mass* for each day of these seasons, lest the "continuous reading" of Scripture be interrupted or readings that express the particular character of a season neglected. But in the case of a celebration that is carried out in the manner of a feast or solemnity, the readings may be taken from those provided in this Lectionary for the various Masses.[4]

b. During Ordinary Time it is up to the priest celebrant "in consultation with the ministers and others who have a function in the celebration, including the faithful"[5] to decide which is more beneficial: to take the readings from the *Collection of Masses* or to take them from the seasonal *Lectionary for Mass.*

II. THE BLESSED VIRGIN MARY, MODEL OF THE CHURCH LISTENING TO THE WORD OF GOD

6   The Church surrounds the proclamation of the word of God in the celebration of Mass with the highest liturgical signs of reverence and reminds the faithful again and again to be "doers of the word, not hearers only" (James 1:22), deceiving themselves. And according to the words of the Lord, they are blessed "who hear the word of God and keep it" (Luke 11:28).

7   Throughout the centuries many holy disciples of the Lord have deeply loved the word of God and turned avidly to the Scriptures as a source of living water. But before all others the Church proposes as the model of the disciple listening to the word of God the Virgin of Nazareth, who, because of her faith, was the first person in the New Testament to be hailed as blessed (see Luke 1:45).

8   The Blessed Virgin listened with faith and welcomed with love the message of the angel Gabriel, so that she who referred to herself as the handmaid of the Lord (see Luke 1:38) became the mother of Christ; she conceived the Son

---

* This reference is to the 1981 edition.

[3] See *Lectionary for Mass* (2nd *editio typica,* 1981), Common of the Blessed Virgin Mary, nos. 707-712; see also vol. 2 of the *Collection of Masses,* Appendix, nos. 1-21.

[4] See the *Collection of Masses of the Blessed Virgin Mary,* vol. 1, Introduction, no. 31 c.

[5] See General Instruction of the Roman Missal, no. 313; English tr., ICEL *Documents on the Liturgy, 1963-1979: Conciliar, Papal, and Curial Texts,* hereafter DOL (The Liturgical Press, Collegeville, Minn., 1982) 208, no. 1703. *Lectionary for Mass* (ed. 1981), General Introduction, no. 78.

in her heart before conceiving him in her womb.[6] Mary, as the prudent virgin, hid the words of God in her heart and, as the wise virgin, turned them over in her mind and dwelt upon them (see Luke 2:19 and 51).

The word of God that took root in her heart moved Mary to visit her cousin Elizabeth, so that together with Elizabeth she might proclaim the greatness of the Lord for his goodness and mercy toward Israel, his beloved servant (see Luke 1:54). The Virgin of Nazareth did not turn away from harsh words (see Luke 2:34-35; Matthew 2:13) or obscure words (see Luke 2:49) spoken to or of her prophetically; rather, fully accepting the plan of God, she kept these words in her heart (see Luke 2:51).

At the wedding feast of Cana Mary understood in the reply of her Son (see John 2:4) something more than the spoken words and she saw more deeply into the meaning of the "miracle of Cana." She therefore instructed the servants to obey the command of the Lord (see John 2:5) and in this way assisted the faith of Jesus' disciples.

Standing at the foot of the cross (see John 19:25), she accepted the words of her Son, who, before he died, entrusted his beloved disciple to her maternal care (see John 19:26). Mary also obeyed the command the risen Lord gave to his apostles, to stay in the city until they had been endowed with power from on high (see Luke 24:49); she remained in Jerusalem and, with one accord continuing in prayer with the apostles, awaited with faith the gift of the Holy Spirit.

9   Thus when the Roman liturgy instructs the faithful about receiving the word of God, it often proposes to them the example of the Blessed Virgin Mary. God made her intent upon his word[7] and Mary, the new Eve, obeyed his word[8] and showed herself docile to the word of her Son.[9] The mother of Jesus is rightly called, therefore, "the Virgin who listens, welcoming the word of God with faith."[10] Following Mary in this "the Church, above all in the liturgy, listens to the word of God, welcomes it, proclaims and reveres it; the Church gives it to Christ's faithful as the bread of life; in the light of that word the Church reads the signs of the times, interprets human events, and lives its life."[11]

10   To the faithful who visit shrines dedicated to the Mother of God or who take part in the memorial of the Blessed Virgin on Saturday pastors should teach the most excellent homage of devotion they can offer the Blessed Virgin: that in liturgical celebrations they proclaim the word of God rightly and revere it with a special love; that they listen to this word with faith and keep it in their hearts; that they dwell upon it inwardly and have it on their lips to share it with others; that they carry it out faithfully and let it shape their entire lives.

---

[6] See Augustine, *Sermo 215*, 4: PL 38, 1074. Leo the Great, *In Nativitate Domini Sermo 1*, I: PL 54, 191.

[7] See *The Liturgy of the Hours*, Common of the Blessed Virgin Mary, Evening Prayer I and II, intercessions, alternate formulary.

[8] See ibid., 25 March, Annunciation, Morning Prayer, intercessions.

[10] Paul VI, Apostolic Exhortation, *Marialis cultus*, no. 17: AAS 66 (1974), p. 128; DOL 467, no. 3915.

[11] Ibid.: AAS 66 (1974), p. 129; DOL 467, no. 3915.

ADVENT SEASON

During Advent the Roman liturgy celebrates the two comings of the Lord: the First Coming in lowliness, when in the fullness of time (see Galatians 4:4) the Lord took flesh of the Blessed Virgin Mary and came into the world to save the human race; the Second Coming in glory, when at the end of time the Lord will come "to judge the living and the dead" (Creed) and to lead the just into the house of his Father, where Mary has preceded them in glory.

MASS FORMULARIES

1. The Blessed Virgin Mary, Chosen Daughter of Israel
2. The Blessed Virgin Mary and the Annunciation of the Lord
3. The Visitation of the Blessed Virgin Mary

1. THE BLESSED VIRGIN MARY, CHOSEN DAUGHTER OF ISRAEL

FIRST READING

A   God spoke to our ancestors, to Abraham and his seed for ever.

A reading from the book of Genesis   12:1-7

The LORD said to Abram:
"Go forth from the land of your kinsfolk
and from your father's house to a land that I will show
you.

"I will make of you a great nation,
and I will bless you;
I will make your name great,
so that you will be a blessing.
I will bless those who bless you
and curse those who curse you.
All the communities of the earth
shall find blessing in you."

Abram went as the LORD directed him, and Lot went with
him.
Abram was seventy-five years old when he left Haran.
Abram took his wife Sarai, his brother's son Lot,
all the possessions that they had accumulated,
and the persons they had acquired in Haran,
and they set out for the land of Canaan.
When they came to the land of Canaan, Abram passed
through the land
as far as the sacred place at Shechem,
by the terebinth of Moreh.
(The Canaanites were then in the land.)

The LORD appeared to Abram and said,
"To your descendants I will give this land."
So Abram built an altar there to the LORD who had ap-
peared to him.

The word of the Lord.

21

B   The Lord God will give to him the throne of his father, David.

A reading from the second book of Samuel   7:1-5, 8b-11, 16

When King David was settled in his palace,
    and the LORD had given him rest from his enemies on
        every side,
    he said to Nathan the prophet,
    "Here I am living in a house of cedar,
    while the ark of God dwells in a tent!"
Nathan answered the king,
    "Go, do whatever you have in mind,
    for the LORD is with you."
But that night the LORD spoke to Nathan and said:
    "Go tell my servant David, 'Thus says the LORD:
    Should you build me a house to dwell in?

" 'It was I who took you from the pasture
    and from the care of the flock
    to be commander of my people Israel.
I have been with you wherever you went,
    and I have destroyed all your enemies before you.
And I will make you famous like the great ones of the earth.
I will fix a place for my people Israel;
    I will plant them so that they may dwell in their place
    without further disturbance.
Neither shall the wicked continue to afflict them as they did
        of old,
    since the time I first appointed judges over my people
        Israel.
I will give you rest from all your enemies.
The LORD also reveals to you
    that he will establish a house for you.
Your house and your kingdom shall endure forever before
        me;
    your throne shall stand firm forever.' "

                                    The word of the Lord.

C   Or reading no. I, 5 in the Appendix, page 207.

RESPONSORIAL PSALM   Psalm 113:1-2, 3-4, 5-6, 7-8

℟. (2) Blessed be the name of the Lord for ever.

Praise, you servants of the LORD,
praise the name of the LORD.
Blessed be the name of the LORD
both now and forever.

℟. Blessed be the name of the Lord for ever.

From the rising of the sun to its setting
let the name of the LORD be praised.
High above all nations is the LORD;
above the heavens God's glory.

℟. Blessed be the name of the Lord for ever.

Who is like the LORD,
our God enthroned on high,
looking down on heaven and earth?

℟. Blessed be the name of the Lord for ever.

The LORD raises the needy from the dust,
lifts the poor from the ash heap,
seats them with princes,
the princes of the people.

℟. Blessed be the name of the Lord for ever.

ALLELUIA

℟. Alleluia, alleluia.

Come, Flower of Jesse's stem,
sign of God's love for all peoples:
save us without delay!

℟. Alleluia.

GOSPEL

A genealogy of Jesus Christ, son of David, son of Abraham.

✠ **A reading from the holy gospel according to Matthew**

1:1-17

The book of the genealogy of Jesus Christ,
  the son of David, the son of Abraham.

Abraham became the father of Isaac,
  Isaac the father of Jacob,
  Jacob the father of Judah and his brothers.
Judah became the father of Perez and Zerah,
  whose mother was Tamar.
Perez became the father of Hezron,
  Hezron the father of Ram,
  Ram the father of Amminadab.
Amminadab became the father of Nahshon,
  Nahshon the father of Salmon,
  Salmon the father of Boaz,
  whose mother was Rahab.
Boaz became the father of Obed,
  whose mother was Ruth.
Obed became the father of Jesse,
  Jesse the father of David the king.

David became the father of Solomon,
  whose mother had been the wife of Uriah.
Solomon became the father of Rehoboam,
  Rehoboam the father of Abijah,
  Abijah the father of Asaph.
Asaph became the father of Jehoshaphat,
  Jehoshaphat the father of Joram,
  Joram the father of Uzziah.
Uzziah became the father of Jotham,
  Jotham the father of Ahaz,
  Ahaz the father of Hezekiah.
Hezekiah became the father of Manasseh,
  Manasseh the father of Amos,
  Amos the father of Josiah.

Josiah became the father of Jechoniah and his brothers
    at the time of the Babylonian exile.
After the Babylonian exile,
    Jechoniah became the father of Shealtiel,
    Shealtiel the father of Zerubbabel,
    Zerubbabel the father of Abiud.
Abiud became the father of Eliakim,
    Eliakim the father of Azor,
    Azor the father of Zadok.
Zadok became the father of Achim,
    Achim the father of Eliud,
    Eliud the father of Eleazar.
Eleazar became the father of Matthan,
    Matthan the father of Jacob,
    Jacob the father of Joseph, the husband of Mary.
Of Mary was born Jesus who is called the Messiah.

Thus the total number of generations
    from Abraham to David
    is fourteen generations;
    from David to the Babylonian exile, fourteen genera-
        tions;
    from the Babylonian exile to the Messiah,
    fourteen generations.

                                 The gospel of the Lord.

2. THE BLESSED VIRGIN MARY AND THE ANNUNCIATION OF THE LORD

FIRST READING

A The virgin will conceive.

A reading from the book of the prophet Isaiah   7:10-14; 8:10c

The LORD spoke to Ahaz:
    Ask for a sign from the LORD, your God;
    let it be deep as the netherworld, or high as the sky!
But Ahaz answered,
    "I will not ask! I will not tempt the LORD!"
Then Isaiah said:
    Listen, O house of David!
Is it not enough for you to weary people,
    must you also weary my God?
Therefore the Lord himself will give you this sign:
    the virgin shall be with child, and bear a son,
    and shall name him Immanuel, which means "With us is
        God!"

The word of the Lord.

B Or reading no. I, 6 in the Appendix, page 209.

RESPONSORIAL PSALM   Psalm 40:7-8a, 8b-9, 10, 11

R̸. (See 8a and 9a) Here am I, Lord; I come to do your will.

Sacrifice and offering you do not want;
but ears open to obedience you gave me.
Holocausts and sin-offerings you do not require;
so I said, "Here I am.

R̸. Here am I, Lord; I come to do your will.

Your commands for me are written in the scroll.
To do your will is my delight;
my God, your law is in my heart!"

R̸. Here am I, Lord; I come to do your will.

I announced your deed to a great assembly;
I did not restrain my lips;
you, LORD, are my witness.

℟. Here am I, Lord; I come to do your will.

Your deed I did not hide within my heart;
your loyal deliverance I have proclaimed.
I made no secret of your enduring kindness
to a great assembly.

℟. Here am I, Lord; I come to do your will.

ALLELUIA   John 1:14ab

℟. Alleluia, alleluia.

The Word of God became flesh and dwelt among us,
and we saw his glory.

℟. Alleluia, alleluia.

GOSPEL

A

You will conceive and bear a son.

✚ A reading from the holy gospel according to Luke   1:26-38

The angel Gabriel was sent from God
    to a town of Galilee called Nazareth,
    to a virgin betrothed to a man named Joseph,
    of the house of David,
    and the virgin's name was Mary.
And coming to Mary, the angel said,
    "Hail, favored one! The Lord is with you."
But Mary was greatly troubled at what was said
    and pondered what sort of greeting this might be.
Then the angel said to her,
    "Do not be afraid, Mary,
    for you have found favor with God.

"Behold, you will conceive in your womb and bear a son,
and you shall name him Jesus.
He will be great and will be called Son of the Most High,
and the Lord God will give him the throne of David his
father,
and he will rule over the house of Jacob forever,
and of his kingdom there will be no end."
But Mary said to the angel,
"How can this be,
since I have no relations with a man?"
And the angel said to her in reply,
"The holy Spirit will come upon you,
and the power of the Most High will overshadow you.
Therefore the child to be born
will be called holy, the Son of God.
And behold, Elizabeth, your relative,
has also conceived a son in her old age,
and this is the sixth month for her who was called
barren;
for nothing will be impossible for God."
Mary said, "Behold, I am the handmaid of the Lord.
May it be done to me according to your word."
Then the angel departed from her.

The gospel of the Lord.

B   Or reading no. III, 17 in the Appendix, page 229.

3. THE VISITATION OF THE BLESSED VIRGIN MARY

FIRST READING

A   The Lord, the King of Israel, is among you.

A reading from the book of the prophet Zephaniah   3:14-18a

Shout for joy, O daughter Zion!
    Sing joyfully, O Israel!
Be glad and exult with all your heart,
    O daughter Jerusalem!
The LORD has removed the judgment against you
    and turned away your enemies;
the King of Israel, the LORD, is in your midst,
    you have no further misfortune to fear.
On that day, it shall be said to Jerusalem:
    Fear not, O Zion, be not discouraged!

The LORD, your God, is in your midst,
    a mighty savior;
the LORD will rejoice over you with gladness,
    and renew you in his love,
the LORD will sing joyfully because of you,
    as one sings at festivals.

                                        The word of the Lord.

B   See, my lover comes leaping across the mountains.

A reading from the Song of Songs   2:8-14

Hark! my lover—here he comes
    springing across the mountains,
    leaping across the hills.
My lover is like a gazelle
    or a young stag.
Here he stands behind our wall,
    gazing through the windows,
    peering through the lattices.
My lover speaks; he says to me,
    "Arise, my beloved, my beautiful one,
    and come!

"For see, the winter is past,
>   the rains are over and gone.
The flowers appear on the earth,
>   the time of pruning the vines has come,
>   and the song of the dove is heard in our land.
The fig tree puts forth its figs,
>   and the vines, in bloom, give forth fragrance.
Arise, my beloved, my beautiful one,
>   and come!
O my dove in the clefts of the rock,
>   in the secret recesses of the cliff,
let me see you,
>   let me hear your voice,
for your voice is sweet,
>   and you are lovely."

The word of the Lord.

C   Or reading no. I, 8 in the Appendix, page 213.

RESPONSORIAL PSALM   Isaiah 12:2-3, 4bcd, 5-6

℟. (6b) Among you is the great and Holy One of Israel.

God indeed is my savior;
I am confident and unafraid.
My strength and my courage is the LORD,
and he has been my savior.
With joy you will draw water
at the fountain of salvation.

℟. Among you is the great and Holy One of Israel.

Give thanks to the LORD, acclaim his name;
among the nations make known his deeds,
proclaim how exalted is his name.

℟. Among you is the great and Holy One of Israel.

Sing praise to the LORD, for his glorious achievement;
let this be known throughout all the earth.
Shout with exultation, O city of Zion,
for great in your midst
is the Holy One of Israel!

℟. Among you is the great and Holy One of Israel.

ALLELUIA   See Luke 1:45

℟. Alleluia, alleluia.

Blessed are you, O Virgin Mary, for firmly believing that the promises of the Lord would be fulfilled.

℟. Alleluia, alleluia.

GOSPEL

Why should I be honored with a visit from the mother of my Lord?

✠ **A reading from the holy gospel according to Luke**   1:39-56

Mary set out
and traveled to the hill country in haste
to a town of Judah,
where she entered the house of Zechariah
and greeted Elizabeth.
**When Elizabeth heard Mary's greeting,
the infant leaped in her womb,
and Elizabeth, filled with the holy Spirit,
cried out in a loud voice and said,
"Most blessed are you among women,
and blessed is the fruit of your womb.
And how does this happen to me,
that the mother of my Lord should come to me?
For at the moment the sound of your greeting reached my
ears,
the infant in my womb leaped for joy.
Blessed are you who believed
that what was spoken to you by the Lord
would be fulfilled."**

**And Mary said:
"My soul proclaims the greatness of the Lord;
my spirit rejoices in God my savior.
For the Lord has looked upon his handmaid's lowliness;
behold, from now on will all ages call me blessed.
The Mighty One has done great things for me,
and holy is his name.**

The Lord's mercy is from age to age
    to those who fear him.
The Lord has shown might with his arm,
    dispersed the arrogant of mind and heart.
The Lord has thrown down the rulers from their thrones
    but lifted up the lowly.
The hungry he has filled with good things;
    the rich he has sent away empty.
The Lord has helped Israel his servant,
    remembering his mercy,
according to his promise to our ancestors,
    to Abraham and to his descendants forever."
Mary remained with Elizabeth about three months
and then returned to her home.

                      The gospel of the Lord.

CHRISTMAS SEASON

During the Christmas season the Church celebrates the mysteries of the childhood of Christ the Savior and his first manifestations. For this reason this liturgical period, though it ends with the feast of the Baptism of the Lord, nevertheless includes the Mass of the Lord's manifestation at the wedding feast of Cana.

In the divine plan the Blessed Virgin was involved in many wonderful ways in the mysteries of the Savior's childhood and manifestations. By a virginal birth she brought forth the Son, showed him to the shepherds and the magi, presented him in the temple and offered him to the Lord. She took her child into exile in Egypt, searched for him when he was lost, and in the home of Nazareth she and Joseph, her husband, led their holy and busy life with Christ. At the wedding feast of Cana she asked a favor of her Son on behalf of the bride and groom and Jesus "performed the first of his signs and manifested his glory" (John 2:11).

MASS FORMULARIES

4. Holy Mary, Mother of God
5. The Blessed Virgin Mary, Mother of the Savior
6. The Blessed Virgin Mary and the Epiphany of the Lord
7. The Blessed Virgin Mary and the Presentation of the Lord
8. Our Lady of Nazareth, I, II
9. Our Lady of Cana

4. HOLY MARY, MOTHER OF GOD

FIRST READING

God sent his Son, born of a woman.

A reading from the letter of Paul to the Galatians   4:4-7

Brothers and sisters:
When the fullness of time had come, God sent his Son,
born of a woman, born under the law,
to ransom those under the law,
so that we might receive adoption.
As proof that you are children,
God sent the spirit of his Son into our hearts,
crying out, "Abba, Father!"
So you are no longer a slave but a child,
and if a child then also an heir, through God.

The word of the Lord.

RESPONSORIAL PSALM   Psalm 22:4-6, 10-11, 23-24

℟. (See 11b) From my mother's womb, O Lord, you are
my God.

Lord, you are enthroned as the Holy One;
you are the glory of Israel.
In you our ancestors trusted;
they trusted and you rescued them.
To you they cried out and they escaped;
in you they trusted and were not disappointed.

℟. From my mother's womb, O Lord, you are my God.

Yet you drew me forth from the womb,
made me safe at my mother's breast.
Upon you I was thrust from the womb;
since birth you are my God.

℟. From my mother's womb, O Lord, you are my God.

Then I will proclaim your name to the assembly;
in the community I will praise you:
"You who fear the Lord, give praise!

All descendants of Jacob, give honor;
show reverence, all descendants of Israel!

℟. From my mother's womb, O Lord, you are my God.

ALLELUIA

℟. Alleluia, alleluia.

**Happy are you, holy Virgin Mary, deserving of all praise;
from you rose the sun of justice, Christ the Lord.**

℟. Alleluia, alleluia.

GOSPEL

The shepherds found Mary and Joseph, and the baby, lying in the manger.

✠ **A reading from the holy gospel according to Luke**   2:15b-19

**The shepherds said to one another,
"Let us go, then, to Bethlehem
to see this thing that has taken place,
that the Lord has made known to us."
So they went in haste and found Mary and Joseph,
and the infant lying in the manger.
When they saw this,
they made known the message
that had been told them about this child.
All who heard it were amazed
by what had been told them by the shepherds.
And Mary kept all these things,
reflecting on them in her heart.**

The gospel of the Lord.

5. THE BLESSED VIRGIN MARY, MOTHER OF THE SAVIOR

FIRST READING

A   A son is given to us.

A reading from the book of the prophet Isaiah   9:1-3, 5-6

The people who walked in darkness
    have seen a great light;
upon those who dwelt in the land of gloom
    a light has shone.
You have brought them abundant joy
    and great rejoicing,
as they rejoice before you as at the harvest,
    as people make merry when dividing spoils.
For the yoke that burdened them,
    the pole on their shoulder,
and the rod of their taskmaster
    you have smashed, as on the day of Midian.
For a child is born to us, a son is given us;
    upon his shoulder dominion rests.
They name him Wonder-Counselor, God-Hero,
    Father-Forever, Prince of Peace.
His dominion is vast
    and forever peaceful,
from David's throne, and over his kingdom,
    which he confirms and sustains
by judgment and justice,
    both now and forever.
The zeal of the LORD of hosts will do this!

The word of the Lord.

B   Or reading no. I, 7 in the Appendix, page 211.

RESPONSORIAL PSALM Psalm 96:1-2a, 2b-3, 11-12, 13

℟. (See Luke 2:11) Our Savior is born, Christ the Lord.

Sing to the LORD **a new song;**
sing to the LORD**, all the earth.**
Sing to the LORD**, bless his name.**

℟. Our Savior is born, Christ the Lord.

Announce salvation day after day.
Tell God's glory among the nations;
among all peoples, God's marvelous deeds.

℟. Our Savior is born, Christ the Lord.

Let the heavens be glad and the earth rejoice;
let the sea and what fills it resound;
let the plains be joyful and all that is in them.
Then let all the trees of the forest rejoice

℟. Our Savior is born, Christ the Lord.

Before the LORD **who comes,**
who comes to govern the earth,
to govern the world with justice
and the peoples with faithfulness.

℟. Our Savior is born, Christ the Lord.

ALLELUIA See Luke 2:10-11

℟. Alleluia, alleluia.

Good news and great joy to all the world:
our Savior is born, Christ the Lord.

℟. Alleluia, alleluia.

GOSPEL

A savior is born for you.

✠ **A reading from the holy gospel according to Luke** 2:1-14

In those days a decree went out from Caesar Augustus
that the whole world should be enrolled.
This was the first enrollment,
when Quirinius was governor of Syria.

So all went to their own towns to be enrolled.
And Joseph too went up from Galilee from the town of
          Nazareth
     to Judea, to the city of David that is called Bethlehem,
     because he was of the house and family of David,
     to be enrolled with Mary, his betrothed, who was with
          child.
While they were there,
     the time came for Mary to have her child,
     and she gave birth to her firstborn son.
She wrapped him in swaddling clothes and laid him in a
          manger,
     because there was no room for them in the inn.

Now there were shepherds in that region living in the fields
     and keeping the night watch over their flock.
The angel of the Lord appeared to them
     and the glory of the Lord shone around them,
     and they were struck with great fear.
The angel said to the shepherds,
     "Do not be afraid;
     for behold, I proclaim to you good news of great joy
     that will be for all the people.
For today in the city of David
     a savior has been born for you who is Messiah and Lord.
And this will be a sign for you:
     you will find an infant wrapped in swaddling clothes
     and lying in a manger."
And suddenly there was a multitude of the heavenly host
          with the angel,
     praising God and saying:
          "Glory to God in the highest
               and on earth peace to those on whom his favor
               rests."

                                        The gospel of the Lord.

6. THE BLESSED VIRGIN MARY AND THE EPIPHANY OF THE LORD

FIRST READING

The glory of the Lord shines upon you.

A reading from the book of the prophet Isaiah   60:1-6

Rise up in splendor, Jerusalem! Your light has come,
   the glory of the Lord shines upon you.
See, darkness covers the earth,
   and thick clouds cover the peoples;
but upon you the LORD shines,
   and over you appears his glory.
Nations shall walk by your light,
   and kings by your shining radiance.
Raise your eyes and look about;
   they all gather and come to you:
your sons come from afar,
   and your daughters in the arms of their nurses.

Then you shall be radiant at what you see,
   your heart shall throb and overflow,
for the riches of the sea shall be emptied out before you,
   the wealth of nations shall be brought to you.
Caravans of camels shall fill you,
   dromedaries from Midian and Ephah;
all from Sheba shall come
   bearing gold and frankincense,
   and proclaiming the praises of the LORD.

The word of the Lord.

RESPONSORIAL PSALM   Psalm 72:1-2, 7-8, 10-11, 12-13

℟. (see 11) Lord, every nation on earth will adore you.

O God, give your judgment to the king;
your justice to the son of kings;
that he may govern your people with justice,
your oppressed with right judgment.

℟. Lord, every nation on earth will adore you.

42

That abundance may flourish in his days,
great bounty, till the moon be no more.
May he rule from sea to sea,
from the river to the ends of the earth.

℟. Lord, every nation on earth will adore you.

May the kings of Tarshish and the islands bring tribute,
the kings of Arabia and Seba offer gifts.
May all kings bow before him,
all nations serve him.

℟. Lord, every nation on earth will adore you.

For he rescues the poor when they cry out,
the oppressed who have no one to help.
He shows pity to the needy and the poor
and saves the lives of the poor.

℟. Lord, every nation on earth will adore you.

ALLELUIA   Matthew 2:2

℟. Alleluia, alleluia.

We have seen his star in the east
and have come to adore the Lord.

℟. Alleluia, alleluia.

GOSPEL

Entering the house, they saw the child with Mary, his mother.

✠ A reading from the holy gospel according to Matthew
                                                               2:1-12

When Jesus was born in Bethlehem of Judea,
   in the days of King Herod,
      behold, magi from the east arrived in Jerusalem, saying,
      "Where is the newborn king of the Jews?
We saw his star at its rising
      and have come to do him homage."
When King Herod heard this,
      he was greatly troubled,
      and all Jerusalem with him.

Assembling all the chief priests and the scribes of the people,
    Herod inquired of them where the Messiah was to be born.
They said to him, "In Bethlehem of Judea,
    for thus it has been written through the prophet:
        'And you, Bethlehem, land of Judah,
            are by no means least among the rulers of Judah;
        since from you shall come a ruler,
            who is to shepherd my people Israel.' "
Then Herod called the magi secretly
    and ascertained from them the time of the star's appearance.
He sent them to Bethlehem and said,
    "Go and search diligently for the child.
When you have found him, bring me word,
    that I too may go and do him homage."
After their audience with the king the magi set out.
And behold, the star that they had seen at its rising preceded them,
    until it came and stopped over the place where the child was.
They were overjoyed at seeing the star,
    and on entering the house
    they saw the child with Mary his mother.
The magi prostrated themselves and did him homage.
Then they opened their treasures
    and offered him gifts of gold, frankincense, and myrrh.
And having been warned in a dream not to return to Herod,
    the magi departed for their country by another way.

                                The gospel of the Lord.

7. THE BLESSED VIRGIN MARY AND THE PRESENTATION OF THE LORD

FIRST READING

The Lord whom you seek will come to his temple.

A reading from the book of the prophet Malachi   3:1-4

The LORD says:
   Lo, I am sending my messenger
   to prepare the way before me;
and suddenly there will come to the temple
   the LORD whom you seek,
and the messenger of the covenant whom you desire.
   Yes, he is coming, says the LORD of hosts.
But who will endure the day of his coming?
   And who can stand when he appears?
For he is like the refiner's fire,
   or like the fuller's lye.
He will sit refining and purifying silver,
   and he will purify the sons of Levi,
refining them like gold or like silver
   that they may offer due sacrifice to the LORD.
Then the sacrifice of Judah and Jerusalem
   will please the LORD,
   as in the days of old, as in years gone by.

The word of the Lord.

RESPONSORIAL PSALM   Psalm 24:7, 8, 9, 10

℟. (10b) The Lord of hosts is king of glory.

Lift up your heads, O gates;
rise up, you ancient portals,
that the king of glory may enter.

℟. The Lord of hosts is king of glory.

Who is this king of glory?
The LORD, a mighty warrior,
the LORD, mighty in battle.

R̦. The Lord of hosts is king of glory.

Lift up your heads, O gates;
rise up, you ancient portals,
that the king of glory may enter.

R̦. The Lord of hosts is king of glory.

Who is this king of glory?
The LORD of hosts is the king of glory.

R̦. The Lord of hosts is king of glory.

ALLELUIA

R̦.   Alleluia, alleluia.

Jesse's shoot has blossomed:
a virgin has given birth
to one who is truly God and truly human;
God has restored our peace,
reconciling in himself earth with heaven.

R̦.   Alleluia, alleluia.

GOSPEL

A sword will pierce your very soul.

✠ A reading from the holy gospel according to Luke   2:27-35

Simeon came in the Spirit into the temple;
and when the parents brought in the child Jesus
to perform the custom of the law in regard to him,
Simeon took Jesus into his arms and blessed God, saying:
"Now, Master, you may let your servant go
in peace, according to your word,
for my eyes have seen your salvation,
which you prepared in sight of all the peoples,
a light for revelation to the Gentiles,
and glory for your people Israel."

The father and mother of Jesus were amazed at what was
        said about him;
    and Simeon blessed them and said to Mary his mother,
    "Behold, this child is destined
    for the fall and rise of many in Israel,
    and to be a sign that will be contradicted
    (and you yourself a sword will pierce)
    so that the thoughts of many hearts may be revealed."

The gospel of the Lord.

8. OUR LADY OF NAZARETH

I

FIRST READING

God sent his Son, born of a woman, born under the law.

A reading from the letter of Paul to the Galatians   4:4-7

Brothers and sisters:
**When the fullness of time had come, God sent his Son,
    born of a woman, born under the law,
    to ransom those under the law,
    so that we might receive adoption.
As proof that you are children,
    God sent the spirit of his Son into our hearts,
    crying out, "Abba, Father!"
So you are no longer a slave but a child,
    and if a child then also an heir, through God.**

The word of the Lord.

RESPONSORIAL PSALM   Psalm 131:1, 2, 3

℟. In you, Lord, I have found my peace.

**LORD, my heart is not proud;
nor are my eyes haughty;
I do not busy myself with great matters,
with things too sublime for me.**

℟. In you, Lord, I have found my peace.

**Rather, I have stilled my soul,
hushed it like a weaned child.
Like a weaned child on its mother's lap,
so is my soul within me.**

℟. In you, Lord, I have found my peace.

**Israel, hope in the LORD,
now and forever.**

℟. In you, Lord, I have found my peace.

48

ALLELUIA

R̸. Alleluia, alleluia.

**Virgin Mother of God,
he whom the whole world cannot contain
enclosed himself as a child within your womb.**

R̸. Alleluia, alleluia.

GOSPEL

A   They returned to their own home of Nazareth. The child grew to maturity, and he was filled with wisdom.

✝ **A reading from the holy gospel according to Luke**

2:22, 39-40

When the days were completed for their purification
according to the law of Moses,
Mary and Joseph took Jesus up to Jerusalem
to present him to the Lord.

**When Mary and Joseph had fulfilled all the prescriptions
of the law of the Lord,
they returned to Galilee,
to their own town of Nazareth.
The child, Jesus, grew and became strong, filled with wisdom;
and the favor of God was upon him.**

The gospel of the Lord.

B   Jesus went down with them and came to Nazareth, where he was subject to them.

✝ **A reading from the holy gospel according to Luke**   2:41-52

Each year Jesus' parents went to Jerusalem for the feast
of Passover,
and when Jesus was twelve years old,
they went up according to festival custom.
After they had completed its days, as they were returning,
the boy Jesus remained behind in Jerusalem,
but his parents did not know it.

Thinking that Jesus was in the caravan,
>they journeyed for a day
>and looked for him among their relatives and acquain-
>>tances,
>but not finding him,
>they returned to Jerusalem to look for him.

After three days they found Jesus in the temple,
>sitting in the midst of the teachers,
>listening to them and asking them questions,
>and all who heard him were astounded
>at his understanding and his answers.

When Jesus' parents saw him,
>they were astonished,
>and his mother said to him,
>"Son, why have you done this to us?

Your father and I have been looking for you with great
>>anxiety."

And Jesus said to them,
>"Why were you looking for me?

Did you not know that I must be in my Father's house?"

But his parents did not understand what he said to them.

Jesus went down with them and came to Nazareth,
>and was obedient to them;
>and his mother kept all these things in her heart.

And Jesus advanced in wisdom and age and favor
>before God and people.

>>>The gospel of the Lord.

II

FIRST READING

May the fullness of Christ's message live within you.

A reading from the letter of Paul to the Colossians   3:12-17

Brothers and sisters:
Put on, as God's chosen ones, holy and beloved,
   heartfelt compassion, kindness, humility, gentleness,
      and patience,
   bearing with one another and forgiving one another,
   if one has a grievance against another;
   as the Lord has forgiven you, so must you also do.
And over all these put on love,
   that is, the bond of perfection.
And let the peace of Christ control your hearts,
   the peace into which you were also called in one body.
And be thankful.
Let the word of Christ dwell in you richly,
   as in all wisdom you teach and admonish one another,
   singing psalms, hymns, and spiritual songs
   with gratitude in your hearts to God.
And whatever you do, in word or in deed,
   do everything in the name of the Lord Jesus,
   giving thanks to God the Father through him.

The word of the Lord.

RESPONSORIAL PSALM   Psalm 84:2-3, 5-6, 9-10

℟. (See 5a) Blessed are they who dwell in your house, O
Lord.

How lovely your dwelling,
O Lord of hosts!
My soul yearns and pines
for the courts of the Lord.
My heart and flesh cry out
for the living God.

℟. Blessed are they who dwell in your house, O Lord.

Happy are those who dwell in your house!
They never cease to praise you.
Happy are those who find refuge in you,
whose hearts are set on pilgrim roads.

℟. Blessed are they who dwell in your house, O Lord.

LORD of hosts, hear my prayer;
listen, God of Jacob.
O God, look kindly on our shield;
look upon the face of your anointed.

℟. Blessed are they who dwell in your house, O Lord.

ALLELUIA
Colossians 3:15a, 16a

℟. Alleluia, alleluia.

May the peace of Christ rule in your hearts
and the fullness of his message live within you.

℟. Alleluia, alleluia.

GOSPEL

He went and lived in a town called Nazareth.

✢ **A reading from the holy gospel according to Matthew**
2:13-15, 19-23

When the magi had departed,
   behold, the angel of the Lord appeared to Joseph in a
      dream and said,
   "Rise, take the child and his mother, flee to Egypt,
   and stay there until I tell you.
Herod is going to search for the child to destroy him."
Joseph rose and took the child and his mother by night
   and departed for Egypt.
He stayed there until the death of Herod,
   that what the Lord had said through the prophet might
      be fulfilled,
   "Out of Egypt I called my son."

When Herod had died, behold,
> the angel of the Lord appeared in a dream
> to Joseph in Egypt and said,
> "Rise, take the child and his mother and go to the land
> > of Israel,
> for those who sought the child's life are dead."

Joseph rose, took the child and his mother,
> and went to the land of Israel.

But when he heard that Archelaus was ruling over Judea
> in place of his father Herod,
> Joseph was afraid to go back there.

And because he had been warned in a dream,
> he departed for the region of Galilee.

Joseph went and dwelt in a town called Nazareth,
> so that what had been spoken through the prophets
> > might be fulfilled,
> "He shall be called a Nazorean."

> > > > > > The gospel of the Lord.

9. OUR LADY OF CANA

FIRST READING

Whatever the Lord has spoken, we will do.

A reading from the book of Exodus 19:3-8a

Moses went up the mountain to God.
    Then the LORD called to him and said,
    "Thus shall you say to the house of Jacob;
    tell the Israelites:
    You have seen for yourselves how I treated the Egyptians
    and how I bore you up on eagle wings
    and brought you here to myself.
Therefore, if you hearken to my voice and keep my covenant,
    you shall be my special possession,
    dearer to me than all other people,
    though all the earth is mine.
You shall be to me a kingdom of priests, a holy nation.
That is what you must tell the Israelites."
So Moses went and summoned the elders of the people.
When he set before them
    all that the LORD had ordered him to tell them,
    the people all answered together,
    "Everything the LORD has said, we will do."

The word of the Lord.

RESPONSORIAL PSALM   Psalm 119:1-2, 10-11, 12 and 14, 15-16

℟. (4) O Lord, you commanded that your precepts be kept with care.

**Happy those whose way is blameless,
who walk by the teaching of the LORD.
Happy those who observe God's decrees,
who seek the Lord with all their heart.**

℟. O Lord, you commanded that your precepts be kept with care.

54

With all my heart I seek you;
do not let me stray from your commands.
In my heart I treasure your promise,
that I may not sin against you.

> ℞. O Lord, you commanded that your precepts be kept
> with care.

Blessed are you, O LORD;
teach me your laws.
I find joy in the way of your decrees
more than in all riches.

> ℞. O Lord, you commanded that your precepts be kept
> with care.

I will ponder your precepts
and consider your paths.
In your laws I take delight;
I will never forget your word.

> ℞. O Lord, you commanded that your precepts be kept
> with care.

ALLELUIA   See Luke 11:27

> ℞. Alleluia, alleluia.

Blessed are they who hear the word of God and keep it.
Blessed is holy Mary who fully obeyed God's will.

> ℞. Alleluia, alleluia.

GOSPEL

Do whatever he tells you.

✠ A reading from the holy gospel according to John   2:1-11

There was a wedding in Cana in Galilee,
  and the mother of Jesus was there.
Jesus and his disciples were also invited to the wedding.
When the wine ran short,
    the mother of Jesus said to him,
    "They have no wine."

And Jesus said to her,
    "Woman, how does your concern affect me?
My hour has not yet come."
His mother said to the servers,
    "Do whatever he tells you."
Now there were six stone water jars there for Jewish cere-
        monial washings,
    each holding twenty to thirty gallons.
Jesus told the servers,
    "Fill the jars with water."
So they filled them to the brim.
Then Jesus told them,
    "Draw some out now and take it to the headwaiter."
So they took it.
And when the headwaiter tasted the water that had become
        wine,
    without knowing where it came from
    (although the servers who had drawn the water knew),
    the headwaiter called the bridegroom and said to him,
    "Everyone serves good wine first,
    and then when people have drunk freely, an inferior
        one;
    but you have kept the good wine until now."
Jesus did this as the beginning of his signs in Cana in
        Galilee
    and so revealed his glory,
    and his disciples began to believe in him.

                            The gospel of the Lord.

LENTEN SEASON

During Lent the faithful are properly prepared to celebrate Easter by hearing the word of God more fully, by spending time in prayer, by doing penance, by recalling their own baptism, and by following Christ along the way of the cross. On this "Lenten journey" the liturgy presents the Blessed Virgin to the faithful as the model of the disciple who faithfully listens to the word of God and follows the footsteps of Christ to Calvary, there to die with him (see 2 Timothy 2:11). At the end of Lent during the Easter triduum the Blessed Virgin is presented to the faithful both as the new Eve or the "new woman" who stands by the tree of life (see John 19:25), as the companion of Christ the "new man," and as the spiritual mother into whose maternal care the Lord entrusts all his followers (see John 19:26).

MASS FORMULARIES

10. Holy Mary, Disciple of the Lord
11. The Blessed Virgin Mary at the Foot of the Cross, I
12. The Blessed Virgin Mary at the Foot of the Cross, II
13. The Commending of the Blessed Virgin Mary
14. The Blessed Virgin Mary, Mother of Reconciliation

10. HOLY MARY, DISCIPLE OF THE LORD

FIRST READING

My heart delighted in wisdom.

A reading from the book of Sirach   51:13-18, 20-22

When I was young and innocent,
     I sought wisdom.
She came to me in her beauty,
     and until the end I will cultivate her.
As the blossoms yielded to ripening grapes,
     the heart's joy,
my feet kept to the level path
     because from earliest youth I was familiar with her.
In the short time I paid heed,
     I met with great instruction.
Since in this way I have profited,
     I will give my teacher grateful praise.
I became resolutely devoted to her—
     the good I persistently strove for.
For her I purified my hands;
     in cleanness I attained to her.
At first acquaintance with her, I gained understanding
     such that I will never forsake her.
My whole being was stirred as I learned about her;
     therefore I have made her my prize possession.
The Lord has granted me my lips as a reward,
     and my tongue will declare his praises.

The word of the Lord.

RESPONSORIAL PSALM   Psalm 19:8-9, 10-11, 15

℞. (See John 6:63c) Your words, Lord, are spirit and life.

The law of the LORD is perfect,
refreshing the soul.
The decree of the LORD is trustworthy,
giving wisdom to the simple.
The precepts of the LORD are right,
rejoicing the heart.

61

The command of the LORD is clear,
enlightening the eye.

> R︥. Your words, Lord, are spirit and life.

The fear of the LORD is pure,
enduring forever.
The statutes of the LORD are true,
all of them just;
more desirable than gold,
than a hoard of purest gold,
sweeter also than honey
or drippings from the comb.

> R︥. Your words, Lord, are spirit and life.

Let the words of my mouth meet with your favor,
keep the thoughts of my heart before you,
LORD, my rock and my redeemer.

> R︥. Your words, Lord, are spirit and life.

VERSE BEFORE THE GOSPEL   See Luke 2:19

**Blessed is the Virgin Mary who kept the word of God
and pondered it in her heart.**

GOSPEL

A   The mother of Jesus treasured all these things in her heart.

✠ A reading from the holy gospel according to Luke   2:41-52

Each year Jesus' parents went to Jerusalem for the feast
         of Passover,
      and when Jesus was twelve years old,
      they went up according to festival custom.
After they had completed its days, as they were returning,
      the boy Jesus remained behind in Jerusalem,
      but his parents did not know it.
Thinking that Jesus was in the caravan,
      they journeyed for a day
      and looked for him among their relatives and acquain-
         tances,
      but not finding him,
      they returned to Jerusalem to look for him.

After three days they found Jesus in the temple,
  sitting in the midst of the teachers,
  listening to them and asking them questions,
  and all who heard him were astounded
  at his understanding and his answers.
When Jesus' parents saw him,
  they were astonished,
  and his mother said to him,
  "Son, why have you done this to us?
Your father and I have been looking for you with great
    anxiety."
And Jesus said to them,
  "Why were you looking for me?
Did you not know that I must be in my Father's house?"
But his parents did not understand what he said to them.
Jesus went down with them and came to Nazareth,
  and was obedient to them;
  and his mother kept all these things in her heart.
And Jesus advanced in wisdom and age and favor
  before God and people.

> The gospel of the Lord.

B Extending his hands toward the disciples, he said: Here are my mother and my brothers.

✤ **A reading from the holy gospel according to Matthew**

12:46-50

While Jesus was speaking to the crowds,
  his mother and his brothers appeared outside,
  wishing to speak with him.
Someone told him, "Your mother and your brothers are
    standing outside,
  asking to speak with you."
But Jesus said in reply to the one who told him,
  "Who is my mother? Who are my brothers?"
And stretching out his hand toward his disciples, he said,
  "Here are my mother and my brothers.
For whoever does the will of my heavenly Father
  is my brother, and sister, and mother."

> The gospel of the Lord.

C Or reading no. III, 19 in the Appendix, page 231.

11. THE BLESSED VIRGIN MARY AT THE FOOT OF THE CROSS

I

FIRST READING

A   God did not spare his own Son.

A reading from the letter of Paul to the Romans   8:31b-39

Brothers and sisters:
If God is for us, who can be against us?
God who did not spare his own Son
    but handed him over for us all,
    how will God not also give us everything else along with
        his Son?
Who will bring a charge against God's chosen ones?
It is God who acquits us.
    Who will condemn?
It is Christ Jesus who died, rather, was raised,
    who also is at the right hand of God,
    who indeed intercedes for us.
Who will separate us from the love of Christ?
Will anguish, or distress, or persecution, or famine,
    or nakedness, or peril, or the sword?
As it is written:
        "For your sake we are being slain all the day;
            we are looked upon as sheep to be slaughtered."
No, in all these things we conquer overwhelmingly
    through Christ Jesus who loved us.
For I am convinced that neither death, nor life,
    nor angels, nor principalities,
    nor present things, nor future things,
    nor powers, nor height, nor depth,
    nor any other creature will be able to separate us
    from the love of God in Christ Jesus our Lord.

The word of the Lord.

B   Or reading no. II, 15 in the Appendix, page 225.

RESPONSORIAL PSALM   Psalm 18:2-3, 5-6, 7, 19-20

℟. (7a) In my distress I called upon the Lord.

I love you, LORD, my strength,
LORD, my rock, my fortress, my deliverer,
my God, my rock of refuge,
my shield, my saving horn, my stronghold!

℟. In my distress I called upon the Lord.

The breakers of death surged round about me;
the menacing floods terrified me.
The cords of Sheol tightened;
the snares of death lay in wait for me.

℟. In my distress I called upon the Lord.

In my distress I called out: LORD!
I cried out to my God.
From his temple he heard my voice;
my cry to him reached his ears.

℟. In my distress I called upon the Lord.

They attacked me on a day of distress,
but the LORD came to my support.
He set me free in the open;
he rescued me because he loves me.

℟. In my distress I called upon the Lord.

VERSE BEFORE THE GOSPEL

There by the cross of our Lord Jesus Christ
stood holy Mary, mournful mother,
queen of heaven and earth.

GOSPEL

There by the cross of Jesus stood his mother.

✠ **A reading from the holy gospel according to John**   19:25-27

Standing by the cross of Jesus were his mother
   and his mother's sister, Mary the wife of Clopas,
   and Mary of Magdala.
When Jesus saw his mother and the disciple whom he loved
     standing beside her,
   he said to his mother, "Woman, behold, your son."
Then he said to the disciple,
   "Behold, your mother."
And from that hour the disciple took her into his home.

       The gospel of the Lord.

12. THE BLESSED VIRGIN MARY AT THE FOOT OF THE CROSS

II

FIRST READING

A   You have averted our ruin before our God.

A reading from the book of Judith   13:17-20

All the people were greatly astonished.
They bowed down and worshiped God, saying with one
     accord,
"Blessed are you, our God,
who today have brought to naught the enemies of your
     people."
Then Uzziah said to her:
"Blessed are you, daughter, by the Most High God,
above all the women on earth;
and blessed be the LORD God,
the creator of heaven and earth,
who guided your blow at the head of the chief of our
     enemies.
Your deed of hope will never be forgotten
     by those who tell of the might of God.
May God make this redound to your everlasting honor,
     rewarding you with blessings,
     because you risked your life
     when your people were being oppressed,
     and you averted our disaster,
     walking uprightly before our God."
And all the people answered, "Amen! Amen!"

                                             The word of the Lord.

B   Or reading no. I, 1 or no. II, 16 in the Appendix, page 199 or 227.

RESPONSORIAL PSALM   Psalm 145:1-2, 4-6, 8-9

℟. (9b) The Lord is merciful to every creature.

I will extol you, my God and king;
I will bless your name forever.

Every day I will bless you;
I will praise your name forever.

R̶/. The Lord is merciful to every creature.

One generation praises your deeds to the next
and proclaims your mighty works.
They speak of the splendor of your majestic glory,
tell of your wonderful deeds.
They speak of your fearsome power,
and attest to your great deeds.

R̶/. The Lord is merciful to every creature.

The LORD is gracious and merciful,
slow to anger and abounding in love.
The LORD is good to all,
compassionate to every creature.

R̶/. The Lord is merciful to every creature.

VERSE BEFORE THE GOSPEL

There by the cross of Jesus stood his mother,
firm in faith, strong in hope, burning with love.

GOSPEL

There by the cross of Jesus stood his mother.

✛ A reading from the holy gospel according to John   19:25-27

S tanding by the cross of Jesus were his mother
      and his mother's sister, Mary the wife of Clopas,
      and Mary of Magdala.
When Jesus saw his mother and the disciple whom he loved
            standing beside her,
      he said to his mother, "Woman, behold, your son."
Then he said to the disciple,
      "Behold, your mother."
And from that hour the disciple took her into his home.

The gospel of the Lord.

13. THE COMMENDING OF THE BLESSED VIRGIN MARY

FIRST READING

Because of her hope in the Lord, this admirable mother bore their deaths with honor.

A reading from the second book of Maccabees   7:1, 20-29

It happened that seven brothers with their mother were arrested
    and tortured with whips and scourges by the king,
    to force them to eat pork in violation of God's law.

Most admirable and worthy of everlasting remembrance was the mother,
    who saw her seven sons perish in a single day,
    yet bore it courageously because of her hope in the LORD.
Filled with a noble spirit that stirred her heart with courage,
    she exhorted each of her sons
    in the language of their ancestors with these words:
    "I do not know how you came into existence in my womb;
    it was not I who gave you the breath of life,
    nor was it I who set in order
    the elements of which each of you is composed.
Therefore, since it is the Creator of the universe
    who shapes each person's beginning,
    as he brings about the origin of everything,
    the Creator, in his mercy,
    will give you back both breath and life,
    because you now disregard yourselves for the sake of his law."

King Antiochus, suspecting insult in her words,
    thought he was being ridiculed.
As the youngest brother was still alive, the king appealed to him,
    not with mere words, but with promises on oath,
    to make him rich and happy if he would abandon his ancestral customs:

the king would make the youngest brother his Friend
and entrust him with high office.
When the youth paid no attention to him at all,
the king appealed to the mother,
urging her to advise her boy to save his life.
After he had urged her for a long time,
she went through the motions of persuading her son.
In derision of the cruel tyrant,
she leaned over close to her son and said in their native
language:
"Son, have pity on me, who carried you in my womb for
nine months,
nursed you for three years, brought you up,
educated and supported you to your present age.
I beg you, child, to look at the heavens and the earth
and see all that is in them;
then you will know that God did not make them out of
existing things;
and in the same way the human race came into existence.
Do not be afraid of this executioner,
but be worthy of your brothers and accept death,
so that in the time of mercy I may receive you again with
them."

The word of the Lord.

RESPONSORIAL PSALM   Psalm 18:2-3, 5-6, 7, 19-20

℟. (7a) In my distress I called upon the Lord.

I love you, LORD, my strength,
LORD, my rock, my fortress, my deliverer,
my God, my rock of refuge,
my shield, my saving horn, my stronghold!

℟. In my distress I called upon the Lord.

The breakers of death surged round about me;
the menacing floods terrified me.
The cords of Sheol tightened;
the snares of death lay in wait for me.

℟. In my distress I called upon the Lord.

In my distress I called out: LORD!
I cried out to my God.
From his temple he heard my voice;
my cry to him reached his ears.

℟. In my distress I called upon the Lord.

They attacked me on a day of distress,
but the LORD came to my support.
He set me free in the open;
he rescued me because he loves you.

℟. In my distress I called upon the Lord.

VERSE BEFORE THE GOSPEL

The mother of Jesus stood by the cross
and tenderly looked on the wounds of her Son,
whose death she knew would redeem the world.

GOSPEL

Woman, this is your son.

✠ A reading from the holy gospel according to John   19:25-27

Standing by the cross of Jesus were his mother
and his mother's sister, Mary the wife of Clopas,
and Mary of Magdala.
When Jesus saw his mother and the disciple whom he loved
standing beside her,
he said to his mother, "Woman, behold, your son."
Then he said to the disciple,
"Behold, your mother."
And from that hour the disciple took her into his home.

The gospel of the Lord.

14. THE BLESSED VIRGIN MARY, MOTHER OF RECONCILIATION

FIRST READING

On behalf of Christ we implore you to be reconciled to God.

A reading from the second letter of Paul to the Corinthians

5:17-21

Brothers and sisters:
Whoever is in Christ is a new creation:
    the old things have passed away;
    behold, new things have come.
And all this is from God,
    who has reconciled us to himself through Christ
    and given us the ministry of reconciliation,
    namely, God was reconciling the world to himself in
        Christ,
    not counting their trespasses against them
    and entrusting to us the message of reconciliation.
So we are ambassadors for Christ,
    as if God were appealing through us.
We implore you on behalf of Christ,
    be reconciled to God.
For our sake God made Christ to be sin who did not know
        sin,
    so that in Christ we might become the righteousness of
        God.

The word of the Lord.

RESPONSORIAL PSALM

Psalm 103:1-2, 3-4, 8-9, 13-14, 17-18a

℟. (1a) O bless the Lord, my soul.

Bless the LORD, my soul;
all my being, bless his holy name!
Bless the LORD, my soul;
do not forget all the gifts of God.

℟. O bless the Lord, my soul.

Who pardons all your sins,
heals all your ills,

72

delivers your life from the pit,
surrounds you with love and compassion.

    ℟. O bless the Lord, my soul.

Merciful and gracious is the LORD,
slow to anger, abounding in kindness.
God does not always rebuke,
nurses no lasting anger.

    ℟. O bless the Lord, my soul.

As a father has compassion on his children,
so the LORD has compassion on the faithful.
For he knows how we are formed,
remembers that we are dust.

    ℟. O bless the Lord, my soul.

But the LORD's kindness is forever
toward the faithful from age to age.
God favors the children's children
of those who keep the covenant.

    ℟. O bless the Lord, my soul.

VERSE BEFORE THE GOSPEL   See Genesis 9:17

    The cross of Christ is the sign of the covenant
    I have established between me and all living things on
        earth.

GOSPEL

This is your son. This is your mother.

✠ A reading from the holy gospel according to John   19:25-27

Standing by the cross of Jesus were his mother
    and his mother's sister, Mary the wife of Clopas,
    and Mary of Magdala.
When Jesus saw his mother and the disciple whom he loved
        standing beside her,
    he said to his mother, "Woman, behold, your son."
Then he said to the disciple,
    "Behold, your mother."
And from that hour the disciple took her into his home.

        The gospel of the Lord.

EASTER SEASON

During the "great Sunday," the fifty-day period in which with joyful exultation the Church celebrates the paschal mystery, the Roman liturgy also commemorates the Mother of Christ as she was filled with joy because of the resurrection of her Son and as she devoted herself to prayer with the apostles in trusting expectation of the gift of the Holy Spirit (see Acts 1:14). When, in fulfillment of its maternal role, the Church celebrates the sacraments of Christian initiation—which are paschal sacraments—it acknowledges the Blessed Virgin as the model of this maternal role. The Church also accepts the mother of Christ as its exemplar and helper in the mission of proclaiming the gospel that Christ entrusted to it after his resurrection from the dead (see Matthew 28:19-20).

Mass Formularies

15. The Blessed Virgin Mary and the Resurrection of the Lord
16. Holy Mary, Fountain of Light and Life
17. Our Lady of the Cenacle
18. The Blessed Virgin Mary, Queen of Apostles

15. THE BLESSED VIRGIN MARY AND THE RESURRECTION OF THE LORD

FIRST READING

I saw the new Jerusalem, as beautiful as a bride all dressed for her husband.

A reading from the book of Revelation   21:1-5a

I, John, saw a new heaven and a new earth.
The former heaven and the former earth had passed
    away,
and the sea was no more.
I also saw the holy city, a new Jerusalem,
    coming down out of heaven from God,
    prepared as a bride adorned for her husband.
I heard a loud voice from the throne saying,
    "Behold, God's dwelling is with the human race.
God will dwell with them and they will be his people
    and God himself will always be with them as their God.
God will wipe every tear from their eyes,
    and there shall be no more death or mourning, wailing
        or pain,
    for the old order has passed away."

The One who sat on the throne said,
    "Behold, I make all things new."

The word of the Lord.

RESPONSORIAL PSALM   Isaiah 61:10a-d and f, 11; 62:2-3

℟. O Mary, you are the city of God in whom justice
    dwells.

I rejoice heartily in the LORD,
in my God is the joy of my soul;
for he has clothed me with a robe of salvation,
and wrapped me in a mantle of justice,
like a bride bedecked with her jewels.

℟. O Mary, you are the city of God in whom justice
    dwells.

As the earth brings forth its plants,
and a garden makes its growth spring up,
so will the Lord GOD make justice and praise
spring up before all the nations.

℟. O Mary, you are the city of God in whom justice dwells.

Nations shall behold your vindication,
and all kings your glory;
you shall be called by a new name
pronounced by the mouth of the LORD.
You shall be a glorious crown in the hand of the LORD,
a royal diadem held by your God.

℟. O Mary, you are the city of God in whom justice dwells.

ALLELUIA

℟. Alleluia, alleluia.

Hail, holy Mary,
as you stood by the cross in sorrow,
you bore the sufferings of your Son
but now you are filled with serenity and joy.

℟. Alleluia, alleluia.

GOSPEL

Tell his disciples that he has risen.

✜ A reading from the holy gospel according to Matthew

28:1-10

After the sabbath, as the first day of the week was dawning,
    Mary Magdalene and the other Mary came to see the tomb.
And behold, there was a great earthquake;
    for an angel of the Lord descended from heaven,
    approached, rolled back the stone, and sat upon it.
The appearance of the angel was like lightning
    and his clothing was white as snow.

The guards were shaken with fear of him
    and became like dead men.
Then the angel said to the women in reply,
    "Do not be afraid!
I know that you are seeking Jesus the crucified.
He is not here, for he has been raised just as he said.
Come and see the place where he lay.
Then go quickly and tell his disciples,
    'He has been raised from the dead,
    and he is going before you to Galilee;
    there you will see him.'
    Behold, I have told you."
Then Mary Magdalene and the other Mary
    went away quickly from the tomb, fearful yet overjoyed,
    and ran to announce the news to Jesus' disciples.
And behold, Jesus met the women on their way and greeted
      them.
They approached, embraced his feet, and did him homage.
Then Jesus said to them, "Do not be afraid.
Go tell my brothers to go to Galilee,
    and there they will see me."

                                   The gospel of the Lord.

16. HOLY MARY, FOUNTAIN OF LIGHT AND LIFE

FIRST READING

Everyone must be baptized in the name of Jesus Christ.

A reading from the Acts of the Apostles   2:14a, 36-40a, 41-42

On the day of Pentecost, Peter stood up with the Eleven,
raised his voice, and proclaimed:
    "Let the whole house of Israel know for certain
    that God has made him both Lord and Messiah,
    this Jesus whom you crucified."

Now when the people heard this, they were cut to the heart,
    and they asked Peter and the other apostles,
    "What are we to do, my brothers?"
Peter said to them,
    "Repent and be baptized, every one of you,
    in the name of Jesus Christ, for the forgiveness of your
        sins;
    and you will receive the gift of the holy Spirit.
For the promise is made to you and to your children
    and to all those far off,
    whomever the Lord our God will call."
Peter testified with many other arguments, and was exhort-
        ing them.
Those who accepted his message were baptized,
    and about three thousand persons were added that day.

They devoted themselves to the teaching of the apostles
    and to the communal life,
    to the breaking of the bread and to the prayers.

The word of the Lord.

RESPONSORIAL PSALM   Psalm 34:2-3, 6-7, 8, 9

℟. (6a) Look to the Lord and be filled with light.

I will bless the LORD at all times;
praise shall be always in my mouth.
My soul will glory in the LORD
that the poor may hear and be glad.

℟. Look to the Lord and be filled with light.

**Look to God that you may be radiant with joy
and your faces may not blush for shame.
In my misfortune I called,
the LORD heard and saved me from all distress.**

℟. Look to the Lord and be filled with light.

**The angel of the LORD, who encamps with them,
delivers all who fear God.**

℟. Look to the Lord and be filled with light.

**Learn to savor how good the LORD is;
happy are those who take refuge in him.**

℟. Look to the Lord and be filled with light.

ALLELUIA

℟. Alleluia, alleluia.

**Happy are you, holy Virgin Mary,
from you rose the sun of justice, Christ the Lord;
whoever follows him will have the light of life.**

℟. Alleluia, alleluia.

GOSPEL

A   I, the light, have come into the world.

✠ **A reading from the holy gospel according to John**   12:44-50

Jesus cried out and said,
   "Whoever believes in me believes not only in me
   but also in the one who sent me,
   and whoever sees me sees the one who sent me.
I came into the world as light,
   so that everyone who believes in me might not remain in
      darkness.
And if any hear my words and do not observe them,
   I do not condemn them,
   for I did not come to condemn the world but to save the
      world.**

Those who reject me and do not accept my words
    have something to judge them: the word that I spoke,
    it will condemn them on the last day,
    because I did not speak on my own,
    but the Father who sent me commanded me what to say
        and speak.
And I know that his commandment is eternal life.
So what I say, I say as the Father told me."

The gospel of the Lord.

B   What is born of the Spirit is spirit.

✠ A reading from the holy gospel according to John   3:1-6

There was a Pharisee named Nicodemus, a ruler of the
    Jews.
He came to Jesus at night and said to him,
    "Rabbi, we know that you are a teacher who has come
        from God,
    for no one can do these signs that you are doing
    unless God is with that person."
Jesus answered and said to him,
    "Amen, amen, I say to you,
    no one can see the kingdom of God without being born
        from above."
Nicodemus said to him,
    "How can a person once grown old be born again?
Surely he cannot reenter his mother's womb and be born
        again, can he?"
Jesus answered,
    "Amen, amen, I say to you,
    no one can enter the kingdom of God
    without being born of water and Spirit.
What is born of flesh is flesh
    and what is born of spirit is spirit."

The gospel of the Lord.

17. OUR LADY OF THE CENACLE

FIRST READING

You will receive the power of the Holy Spirit.

A reading from the Acts of the Apostles   1:6-14

After the resurrection of Jesus,
the apostles gathered around him and asked,
    "Lord, are you at this time going to restore the kingdom
        to Israel?"
Jesus answered them,
    "It is not for you to know the times or seasons
    that the Father has established by his own authority.
But you will receive power when the holy Spirit comes upon
        you,
    and you will be my witnesses in Jerusalem,
    throughout Judea and Samaria,
    and to the ends of the earth."
When Jesus had said this, as the apostles were looking on,
    he was lifted up, and a cloud took him from their sight.
While the apostles were looking intently at the sky as Jesus
        was going,
    suddenly two men dressed in white garments stood
        beside them.
They said, "Men of Galilee,
    why are you standing there looking at the sky?
This Jesus who has been taken up from you into heaven
    will return in the same way as you have seen him going
        into heaven."
Then the apostles returned to Jerusalem
    from the mount called Olivet, which is near Jerusalem,
    a sabbath day's journey away.

When the apostles entered the city
    they went to the upper room where they were staying,
    Peter and John and James and Andrew,
    Philip and Thomas, Bartholomew and Matthew,
    James son of Alphaeus, Simon the Zealot,
    and Judas son of James.

All these devoted themselves with one accord to prayer,
together with some women,
and Mary the mother of Jesus, and his brothers.

The word of the Lord.

RESPONSORIAL PSALM   Psalm 87:1-2, 3 and 5, 6-7

℟. (3) Glorious things are told of you, O city of God.

The LORD loves the city
founded on holy mountains,
loves the gates of Zion
more than any dwelling in Jacob.

℟. Glorious things are told of you, O city of God.

Glorious things are said of you,
O city of God!
But of Zion it must be said:
"They all were born here."

℟. Glorious things are told of you, O city of God.

The Most High confirms this;
the LORD notes in the register of the peoples:
"This one was born right here."
So all sing in their festive dance:
"Within you is my true home."

℟. Glorious things are told of you, O city of God.

ALLELUIA   See Luke 2:19

℟. Alleluia, alleluia.

Blessed is the Virgin Mary who kept the word of God
and pondered it in her heart.

℟. Alleluia, alleluia.

GOSPEL

A

My mother and my brothers are those who hear the word of God and put it into practice.

✝ **A reading from the holy gospel according to Luke**   8:19-21

The mother of Jesus and his brothers came to Jesus
   but were unable to join him because of the crowd.
He was told,
   "Your mother and your brothers are standing outside
   and they wish to see you."
Jesus said to them in reply,
   "My mother and my brothers are those
   who hear the word of God and act on it."

The gospel of the Lord.

B   Or reading no. III, 21 in the Appendix, page 233.

18. THE BLESSED VIRGIN MARY, QUEEN OF APOSTLES

FIRST READING

With one heart the disciples continued in steadfast prayer with Mary, the mother of Jesus.

A reading from the Acts of the Apostles   1:12-14; 2:1-4

After Jesus had been taken up into heaven,
　the apostles returned to Jerusalem
　from the mount called Olivet, which is near Jerusalem,
　a sabbath day's journey away.

When the apostles entered the city
　they went to the upper room where they were staying,
　Peter and John and James and Andrew,
　Philip and Thomas, Bartholomew and Matthew,
　James son of Alphaeus, Simon the Zealot,
　and Judas son of James.
All these devoted themselves with one accord to prayer,
　together with some women,
　and Mary the mother of Jesus, and his brothers.

When the time for Pentecost was fulfilled,
　the apostles were all in one place together.
And suddenly there came from the sky
　a noise like a strong driving wind,
　and it filled the entire house in which they were.
Then there appeared to them tongues as of fire,
　which parted and came to rest on each one of them.
And they were all filled with the holy Spirit
　and began to speak in different tongues,
　as the Spirit enabled them to proclaim.

　　　　　　　　　　　　　　　　　　　The word of the Lord.

RESPONSORIAL PSALM   Psalm 87:1-2, 3 and 5, 6-7

℟. (3) Glorious things are told of you, O city of God.

The LORD loves the city
founded on holy mountains,

loves the gates of Zion
more than any dwelling in Jacob.

℟. Glorious things are told of you, O city of God.

Glorious things are said of you,
O city of God!
But of Zion it must be said:
"They all were born right here."

℟. Glorious things are told of you, O city of God.

The Most High confirms this;
the LORD notes in the register of the peoples:
"This one was born here."
So all sing in their festive dance:
"Within you is my true home."

℟. Glorious things are told of you, O city of God.

ALLELUIA

℟. Alleluia, alleluia.

There by the cross of our Lord Jesus Christ
stood holy Mary, mournful mother,
queen of heaven and earth.

℟. Alleluia, alleluia.

GOSPEL

Woman, this is your son. This is your mother.

✠ A reading from the holy gospel according to John   19:25-27

Standing by the cross of Jesus were his mother
and his mother's sister, Mary the wife of Clopas,
and Mary of Magdala.
When Jesus saw his mother and the disciple whom he loved
standing beside her,
he said to his mother, "Woman, behold, your son."
Then he said to the disciple,
"Behold, your mother."
And from that hour the disciple took her into his home.

The gospel of the Lord.

ORDINARY TIME

During Ordinary Time memorials of the Blessed Virgin occur frequently both in the General Roman Calendar and in the calendars of the particular Churches and of religious institutes. There are consequently a great number of Marian Mass formularies in propers of the Roman rite, which have one and the same object—the work God has accomplished in Mary in relationship to Christ and the Church—but which celebrate it under its many different aspects.

In view of the mystery that they celebrate the Mass formularies for Ordinary Time are divided into three sections. The first section contains eleven formularies to celebrate memorials of the Mother of God under titles that are derived chiefly from Sacred Scripture or that express Mary's bond with the Church. The second section contains nine formularies to celebrate memorials of the Blessed Virgin Mary under titles that refer to her cooperation in fostering the spiritual life of the faithful. The third section contains eight formularies to celebrate memorials of the Blessed Virgin under titles that suggest her compassionate intercession on behalf of the faithful" (see *Collection of Masses of the Blessed Virgin Mary*, Introduction, no. 24).

SECTION 1

This section contains eleven Mass formularies for the celebration of a memorial of the Mother of God under titles that are chiefly derived from Scripture or that bring out Mary's bond with the Church.

MASS FORMULARIES

19. Holy Mary, Mother of the Lord
20. Holy Mary, the New Eve
21. The Holy Name of the Blessed Virgin Mary
22. Holy Mary, Handmaid of the Lord
23. The Blessed Virgin Mary, Temple of the Lord
24. The Blessed Virgin Mary, Seat of Wisdom
25. The Blessed Virgin Mary, Image and Mother of the Church, I
26. The Blessed Virgin Mary, Image and Mother of the Church, II
27. The Blessed Virgin Mary, Image and Mother of the Church, III
28. The Immaculate Heart of the Blessed Virgin Mary
29. The Blessed Virgin Mary, Queen of All Creation

19. HOLY MARY, MOTHER OF THE LORD

FIRST READING

A   Mary, whose womb bore the Lord, is hailed as the ark of the Lord.

A reading from the first book of Chronicles   15:3-4, 15-16; 16:1-2

David assembled all Israel in Jerusalem to bring the ark
    of the LORD
  to the place which he had prepared for it.
David also called together the descendants of Aaron and the
    Levites.

The Levites bore the ark of God on their shoulders with
    poles,
  as Moses had ordained according to the word of the
    LORD.

David commanded the chiefs of the Levites
  to appoint their relatives as chanters,
  to play on musical instruments, harps, lyres, and cym-
    bals
  to make a loud sound of rejoicing.

They brought in the ark of God and set it within the tent
  which David had pitched for it.
Then they offered up holocausts and peace offerings to God.
When David had finished offering up the holocausts and
    peace offerings,
  he blessed the people in the name of the Lord.

The word of the Lord.

B   Or reading no. I, 3 in the Appendix, page 203.

RESPONSORIAL PSALM   Psalm 132:11, 13-14, 17-18

℞. (11b) I will set on your throne a son, the fruit of your
    womb.

The LORD swore an oath to David,
a pledge never to be broken:
"Your own offspring
I will set upon your throne."

℟. I will set on your throne a son, the fruit of your womb.

Yes, the LORD has chosen Zion,
desired it for a dwelling:
"This is my resting place forever;
here I will dwell, for I desire it.

℟. I will set on your throne a son, the fruit of your womb.

There I will make a horn sprout for David's line;
I will set a lamp for my anointed.
His foes I will clothe with shame,
but on him my crown shall gleam."

℟. I will set on your throne a son, the fruit of your womb.

ALLELUIA

℟. Alleluia, alleluia.

Virgin Mother of God,
he whom the whole world cannot contain
enclosed himself as a child within your womb.

℟. Alleluia, alleluia.

GOSPEL

Blessed is the fruit of your womb.

✠ **A reading from the holy gospel according to Luke**   1:39-47

Mary set out
and traveled to the hill country in haste
to a town of Judah,
where she entered the house of Zechariah
and greeted Elizabeth.
When Elizabeth heard Mary's greeting,
the infant leaped in her womb,
and Elizabeth, filled with the holy Spirit,
cried out in a loud voice and said,
"Most blessed are you among women,
and blessed is the fruit of your womb.

And how does this happen to me,
> that the mother of my Lord should come to me?

For at the moment the sound of your greeting reached my
> ears,

> the infant in my womb leaped for joy.

Blessed are you who believed
> that what was spoken to you by the Lord
> would be fulfilled."

And Mary said:
> "My soul proclaims the greatness of the Lord;
> > my spirit rejoices in God my savior."

The gospel of the Lord.

20. HOLY MARY, THE NEW EVE

FIRST READING

A

I saw the new Jerusalem, as beautiful as a bride all dressed for her husband.

A reading from the book of Revelation   21:1-5a

I, John, saw a new heaven and a new earth.
    The former heaven and the former earth had passed
       away,
    and the sea was no more.
I also saw the holy city, a new Jerusalem,
    coming down out of heaven from God,
    prepared as a bride adorned for her husband.
I heard a loud voice from the throne saying,
    "Behold, God's dwelling is with the human race.
God will dwell with them and they will be his people
    and God himself will always be with them as their God.
God will wipe every tear from their eyes,
    and there shall be no more death or mourning, wailing
       or pain,
    for the old order has passed away."

The One who sat on the throne said,
    "Behold, I make all things new."

                   The word of the Lord.

B

Or reading no. II, 9 or no. II, 14 in the Appendix, page 215 or 223.

RESPONSORIAL PSALM   Isaiah 61:10a-d and f, 11; 62:2-3

℟. O Mary, you are the new earth in whom justice
    dwells.

I rejoice heartily in the LORD,
in my God is the joy of my soul;
for he has clothed me with a robe of salvation,
and wrapped me in a mantle of justice,
like a bride bedecked with her jewels.

℟. O Mary, you are the new earth in whom justice
     dwells.

As the earth brings forth its plants,
and a garden makes its growth spring up,
so will the Lord GOD make justice and praise
spring up before all the nations.

℟. O Mary, you are the new earth in whom justice
     dwells.

Nations shall behold your vindication,
and all kings your glory;
you shall be called by a new name
pronounced by the mouth of the LORD.
You shall be a glorious crown in the hand of the LORD,
a royal diadem held by your God.

℟. O Mary, you are the new earth in whom justice
     dwells.

ALLELUIA

℟. Alleluia, alleluia.

Glorious are you, holy Mary, the new Eve.
From you the new Adam, Christ Jesus, was born.

℟. Alleluia, alleluia.

GOSPEL

A   Hail, full of grace.

✠ A reading from the holy gospel according to Luke   1:26-38

The angel Gabriel was sent from God
     to a town of Galilee called Nazareth,
     to a virgin betrothed to a man named Joseph,
     of the house of David,
     and the virgin's name was Mary.
And coming to Mary, the angel said,
     "Hail, favored one! The Lord is with you."
But Mary was greatly troubled at what was said
     and pondered what sort of greeting this might be.

Then the angel said to her,
    "Do not be afraid, Mary,
    for you have found favor with God.
"Behold, you will conceive in your womb and bear a son,
    and you shall name him Jesus.
He will be great and will be called Son of the Most High,
    and the Lord God will give him the throne of David his
        father,
    and he will rule over the house of Jacob forever,
    and of his kingdom there will be no end."
But Mary said to the angel,
    "How can this be,
    since I have no relations with a man?"
And the angel said to her in reply,
    "The holy Spirit will come upon you,
    and the power of the Most High will overshadow you.
Therefore the child to be born
    will be called holy, the Son of God.
And behold, Elizabeth, your relative,
    has also conceived a son in her old age,
    and this is the sixth month for her who was called
        barren;
    for nothing will be impossible for God."
Mary said, "Behold, I am the handmaid of the Lord.
May it be done to me according to your word."
Then the angel departed from her.

                                          The gospel of the Lord.

B   The mother of Jesus said to the attendants: Do whatever he tells you.

✛ **A reading from the holy gospel according to John** 2:1-11

There was a wedding in Cana in Galilee,
    and the mother of Jesus was there.
Jesus and his disciples were also invited to the wedding.
When the wine ran short,
    the mother of Jesus said to him,
    "They have no wine."

And Jesus said to her,
 "Woman, how does your concern affect me?
My hour has not yet come."
His mother said to the servers,
 "Do whatever he tells you."
Now there were six stone water jars there for Jewish cere-
  monial washings,
 each holding twenty to thirty gallons.
Jesus told the servers,
 "Fill the jars with water."
So they filled them to the brim.
Then Jesus told them,
 "Draw some out now and take it to the headwaiter."
So they took it.
And when the headwaiter tasted the water that had become
  wine,
 without knowing where it came from
 (although the servers who had drawn the water knew),
 the headwaiter called the bridegroom and said to him,
 "Everyone serves good wine first,
 and then when people have drunk freely, an inferior
  one;
 but you have kept the good wine until now."
Jesus did this as the beginning of his signs in Cana in
  Galilee
 and so revealed his glory,
 and his disciples began to believe in him.

         The gospel of the Lord.

21. THE HOLY NAME OF THE BLESSED VIRGIN MARY

FIRST READING

Remembrance of me is a legacy to future generations.

A reading from the book of Sirach   24:17-21

I bud forth delights like the vine,
  my blossoms become fruit fair and rich.
Come to me, all you that yearn for me,
  and be filled with my fruits.
You will remember me as sweeter than honey,
  better to have than the honeycomb.
Whoever eats of me will hunger still,
  whoever drinks of me will thirst for more;
whoever obeys me will not be put to shame,
  whoever serves me will never fail.

The word of the Lord.

RESPONSORIAL PSALM   Luke 1:46-48, 49-50, 53-54

℟. (See Isaiah 61:10b) My spirit rejoices in my God.

My soul proclaims the greatness of the Lord;
my spirit rejoices in God my savior.
For he has looked upon his handmaid's lowliness;
behold, from now on will all ages call me blessed.

℟. My spirit rejoices in my God.

The Mighty One has done great things for me,
and holy is his name.
The Lord's mercy is from age to age
to those who fear him.

℟. My spirit rejoices in my God.

The hungry he has filled with good things;
the rich he has sent away empty.
The Lord has helped Israel his servant,
remembering his mercy.

℟. My spirit rejoices in my God.

ALLELUIA   See Luke 1:28

℟. Alleluia, alleluia.

**Hail, Mary, full of grace, the Lord is with you;
blessed are you among women.**

℟. Alleluia, alleluia.

GOSPEL

The virgin's name was Mary.

✠ A reading from the holy gospel according to Luke   1:26-38

The angel Gabriel was sent from God
    to a town of Galilee called Nazareth,
    to a virgin betrothed to a man named Joseph,
    of the house of David,
    and the virgin's name was Mary.
And coming to Mary, the angel said,
    "Hail, favored one! The Lord is with you."
But Mary was greatly troubled at what was said
    and pondered what sort of greeting this might be.
Then the angel said to her,
    "Do not be afraid, Mary,
    for you have found favor with God.

"Behold, you will conceive in your womb and bear a son,
    and you shall name him Jesus.
He will be great and will be called Son of the Most High,
    and the Lord God will give him the throne of David his
        father,
    and he will rule over the house of Jacob forever,
    and of his kingdom there will be no end."
But Mary said to the angel,
    "How can this be,
    since I have no relations with a man?"
And the angel said to her in reply,
    "The holy Spirit will come upon you,
    and the power of the Most High will overshadow you.
Therefore the child to be born
    will be called holy, the Son of God.

And behold, Elizabeth, your relative,
  has also conceived a son in her old age,
  and this is the sixth month for her who was called
    barren;
  for nothing will be impossible for God."
Mary said, "Behold, I am the handmaid of the Lord.
May it be done to me according to your word."
Then the angel departed from her.

The gospel of the Lord.

22. HOLY MARY, HANDMAID OF THE LORD

I stood praying to the Lord, and the Lord granted my request.

A reading from the first book of Samuel   1:24-28; 2:1-2, 4-8

Hannah brought Samuel with her,
    along with a three-year-old bull,
    an ephah of flour, and a skin of wine,
    and presented him at the temple of the LORD in Shiloh.
After the boy's father had sacrificed the young bull,
    Hannah, his mother, approached Eli and said;
    "Pardon, my lord!
As you live, my lord,
    I am the woman who stood near you here, praying to the
        LORD.
I prayed for this child, and the LORD granted my request.
Now I, in turn, give him to the LORD;
    as long as he lives, he shall be dedicated to the LORD."
Hannah left Samuel there;
    and as she worshiped the LORD, she said:
    "My heart exults in the LORD,
        my horn is exalted in my God.
I have swallowed up my enemies;
    I rejoice in my victory.
There is no Holy One like the LORD;
    there is no Rock like our God.

"The bows of the mighty are broken,
    while the tottering gird on strength.
The well-fed hire themselves out for bread,
    while the hungry batten on spoil.
The barren wife bears seven sons,
    while the mother of many languishes.

"The Lord puts to death and gives life;
    he casts down to the netherworld;
    he raises up again.
The LORD makes poor and makes rich,
    he humbles, he also exalts.

He raises the needy from the dust;
    from the ash heap he lifts up the poor,
to seat them with nobles
    and make a glorious throne their heritage.
He gives to vowers their vows,
    and blesses the sleep of the just.

"For the pillars of the earth are the Lord's,
    and he has set the world upon them."

The word of the Lord.

RESPONSORIAL PSALM   Luke 1:46-48a, 48b-49, 50-51, 52-53, 54-55

R̶. (See 48a) The Lord has looked with favor on his lowly servant.

My soul proclaims the greatness of the Lord;
my spirit rejoices in God my savior.
For he has looked upon his handmaid's lowliness;

R̶. The Lord has looked with favor on his lowly servant.

Behold, from now on will all ages call me blessed.
The Mighty One has done great things for me,
and holy is his name.

R̶. The Lord has looked with favor on his lowly servant.

The Lord's mercy is from age to age
to those who fear him.
He has shown might with his arm,
dispersed the arrogant of mind and heart.

R̶. The Lord has looked with favor on his lowly servant.

He has thrown down the rulers from their thrones
but lifted up the lowly.
The hungry he has filled with good things;
the rich he has sent away empty.

R̶. The Lord has looked with favor on his lowly servant.

The Lord has helped Israel his servant,
remembering his mercy,
according to his promise to our ancestors,
to Abraham and to his descendants for ever.

R̶. The Lord has looked with favor on his lowly servant.

23. THE BLESSED VIRGIN MARY, TEMPLE OF THE LORD

A   A cloud filled the temple of the Lord God.

A reading from the first book of Kings   8:1, 3-7, 9-11

The elders of Israel and all the leaders of the tribes,
   the princes in the ancestral houses of the Israelites,
   came to King Solomon in Jerusalem,
   to bring up the ark of the LORD's covenant
   from the City of David, which is Zion.
When all the elders of Israel had arrived,
   the priests took up the ark;
   they carried the ark of the LORD
   and the meeting tent with all the sacred vessels
   that were in the tent.
(The priests and Levites carried them.)

King Solomon and the entire community of Israel
   present for the occasion
   sacrificed before the ark sheep and oxen
   too many to number or count.
The priests brought the ark of the covenant of the LORD
   to its place beneath the wings of the cherubim in the
      sanctuary,
   the holy of holies of the temple.
The cherubim had their wings spread out over the place of
      the ark,
   sheltering the ark and its poles from above.
There was nothing in the ark but the two stone tablets
   which Moses had put there at Horeb,
   when the LORD made a covenant with the Israelites
   at their departure from the land of Egypt.

When the priests left the holy place,
   the cloud filled the temple of the LORD
   so that the priests could no longer minister because of
      the cloud,
   since the LORD's glory had filled the temple of the LORD.

The word of the Lord.

B   Here God lives among his people.

A reading from the book of Revelation   21:1-5a

I, John, saw a new heaven and a new earth.
     The former heaven and the former earth had passed
          away,
     and the sea was no more.
I also saw the holy city, a new Jerusalem,
     coming down out of heaven from God,
     prepared as a bride adorned for her husband.
I heard a loud voice from the throne saying,
     "Behold, God's dwelling is with the human race.
God will dwell with them and they will be his people
     and God himself will always be with them as their God.
God will wipe every tear from their eyes,
     and there shall be no more death or mourning, wailing
          or pain,
     for the old order has passed away."

The One who sat on the throne said,
     "Behold, I make all things new."

                         The word of the Lord.

C   Or reading no. I, 2 in the Appendix, page 201.

RESPONSORIAL PSALM   Psalm 84:3, 4, 5 and 10, 11

℟. (Revelation 21:3b) Here God lives among his people.

**My soul yearns and pines
for the courts of the LORD.
My heart and flesh cry out
for the living God.**

℟. Here God lives among his people.

**As the sparrow finds a home
and the swallow a nest to settle her young,
my home is by your altars,
LORD of hosts, my king and my God!**

℟. Here God lives among his people.

Happy are those who dwell in your house!
They never cease to praise you.
O God, look kindly on our shield;
look upon the face of your anointed.

℟. Here God lives among his people.

Better one day in your courts
than a thousand elsewhere.
Better the threshold of the house of my God
than a home in the tents of the wicked.

℟. Here God lives among his people.

ALLELUIA

℟. Alleluia, alleluia.

Hail, holy Mary, temple of holiness
and temple of love for us sinners.
Hail, temple filled with the Holy Spirit,
which God the Father chose for the Son.

℟. Alleluia, alleluia.

GOSPEL

The power of the Most High will overshadow you.

✠ A reading from the holy gospel according to Luke   1:26-38

The angel Gabriel was sent from God
    to a town of Galilee called Nazareth,
    to a virgin betrothed to a man named Joseph,
    of the house of David,
    and the virgin's name was Mary.
And coming to Mary, the angel said,
    "Hail, favored one! The Lord is with you."
But Mary was greatly troubled at what was said
    and pondered what sort of greeting this might be.
Then the angel said to her,
    "Do not be afraid, Mary,
    for you have found favor with God.

"Behold, you will conceive in your womb and bear a son,
  and you shall name him Jesus.
He will be great and will be called Son of the Most High,
  and the Lord God will give him the throne of David his
    father,
  and he will rule over the house of Jacob forever,
  and of his kingdom there will be no end."
But Mary said to the angel,
  "How can this be,
  since I have no relations with a man?"
And the angel said to her in reply,
  "The holy Spirit will come upon you,
  and the power of the Most High will overshadow you.
Therefore the child to be born
  will be called holy, the Son of God.
And behold, Elizabeth, your relative,
  has also conceived a son in her old age,
  and this is the sixth month for her who was called
    barren;
  for nothing will be impossible for God."
Mary said, "Behold, I am the handmaid of the Lord.
May it be done to me according to your word."
Then the angel departed from her.

The gospel of the Lord.

24. THE BLESSED VIRGIN MARY, SEAT OF WISDOM

A   Mary, seat of Wisdom.

A reading from the book of Proverbs   8:22-31

Wisdom says:
    "The LORD begot me, the firstborn of his ways,
    the forerunner of his prodigies of long ago;
from of old I was poured forth,
    at the first, before the earth.
When there were no depths I was brought forth,
    when there were no fountains or springs of water;
before the mountains were settled into place,
    before the hills, I was brought forth;
while as yet the earth and fields were not made,
    nor the first clods of the world.

"When the LORD established the heavens I was there,
    when he marked out the vault over the face of the deep;
when the LORD made firm the skies above,
    when he fixed fast the foundations of the earth;
when the LORD set for the sea its limit,
    so that the waters should not transgress his command;
then was I beside the LORD as his craftsman,
    and I was his delight day by day,
playing before him all the while,
    playing on the surface of his earth;
    and I found delight in the children of men."

                                    The word of the Lord.

B   Mary, seat of Wisdom.

A reading from the book of Sirach   24:1-4, 18-21

Wisdom sings her own praises,
    before her own people she proclaims her glory:
in the assembly of the Most HIgh she opens her mouth,
    in the presence of his hosts she declares her worth:

"From the mouth of the Most High I came forth,
    and mistlike covered the earth.
In the highest heavens did I dwell,
    my throne on a pillar of cloud.

"Then the Creator of all gave me his command,
    and my Creator who formed me chose the spot for my
        tent,
saying, 'In Jacob make your dwelling,
    in Israel your inheritance.'
Before all ages, in the beginning, God created me,
    and through all ages I shall not cease to be.
In the holy tent I ministered before him,
    and in Zion I fixed my abode.
Thus in the chosen city God has given me rest,
    in Jerusalem is my domain.
I have struck root among the glorious people,
    in the portion of the Lord, his heritage.

"Come to me, all you that yearn for me,
    and be filled with my fruits;
you will remember me as sweeter than honey,
    better to have than the honeycomb.
Whoever eats of me will hunger still,
    whoever drinks of me will thirst for more;
whoever obeys me will not be put to shame,
    whoever serves me will never fail."

                                    The word of the Lord.

RESPONSORIAL PSALM   Psalm 147:12-13, 14-15, 19-20

℞. (John 1:14) The Word became flesh and dwelt among
    us.

Glorify the LORD, Jerusalem;
Zion, offer praise to your God.

Who has strengthened the bars of your gates,
blessed your children within you,

℟. The Word became flesh and dwelt among us.

Brought peace to your borders,
and filled you to overflowing with finest wheat.
The LORD sends a command earthward;
his word runs swiftly!

℟. The Word became flesh and dwelt among us.

The LORD also proclaims his word to Jacob,
decrees and laws to Israel.
God has not done this for other nations;
of such laws they know nothing.

℟. The Word became flesh and dwelt among us.

ALLELUIA

℟. Alleluia, alleluia.

O happy Virgin, you gave birth to the Lord;
O blessed seat of Wisdom, you cradle in our hearts
the Spirit of your Son Jesus Christ.

℟. Alleluia, alleluia.

GOSPEL

A   Entering the house, they saw the child with Mary, his mother.

✠ A reading from the holy gospel according to Matthew

2:1-12

When Jesus was born in Bethlehem of Judea,
in the days of King Herod,
behold, magi from the east arrived in Jerusalem, saying,
"Where is the newborn king of the Jews?
We saw his star at its rising
and have come to do him homage."
When King Herod heard this,
he was greatly troubled,
and all Jerusalem with him.
Assembling all the chief priests and the scribes of the people,
Herod inquired of them where the Messiah was to be born.

They said to him, "In Bethlehem of Judea,
> for thus it has been written through the prophet:
>> 'And you, Bethlehem, land of Judah,
>>> are by no means least among the rulers of Judah;
>> since from you shall come a ruler,
>>> who is to shepherd my people Israel.' "
Then Herod called the magi secretly
> and ascertained from them the time of the star's appearance.
He sent them to Bethlehem and said,
> "Go and search diligently for the child.
When you have found him, bring me word,
> that I too may go and do him homage."
After their audience with the king the magi set out.
And behold, the star that they had seen at its rising preceded them,
> until it came and stopped over the place where the child was.
They were overjoyed at seeing the star,
> and on entering the house
> they saw the child with Mary his mother.
The magi prostrated themselves and did him homage.
Then they opened their treasures
> and offered him gifts of gold, frankincense, and myrrh.
And having been warned in a dream not to return to Herod,
> the magi departed for their country by another way.

> > > > > > The gospel of the Lord.

B   Mary treasured all these things and pondered them in her heart.

✛ **A reading from the holy gospel according to Luke**   2:15b-19

The shepherds said to one another,
> "Let us go, then, to Bethlehem
> to see this thing that has taken place,
> that the Lord has made known to us."
So they went in haste and found Mary and Joseph,
> and the infant lying in the manger.

When they saw this,
> they made known the message
> that had been told them about this child.

All who heard it were amazed
> by what had been told them by the shepherds.

And Mary kept all these things,
> reflecting on them in her heart.

The gospel of the Lord.

C

Mary chose the better part.

✠ **A reading from the holy gospel according to Luke**   10:38-42

Jesus entered a village
> where a woman whose name was Martha welcomed
> him.

She had a sister named Mary
> who sat beside the Lord at his feet listening to him
> speak.

Martha, burdened with much serving, came to Jesus and
> said,

> "Lord, do you not care
> that my sister has left me by myself to do the serving?

Tell her to help me."

The Lord said to Martha in reply,

> "Martha, Martha, you are anxious and worried about
> many things.

There is need of only one thing.

Mary has chosen the better part
> and it will not be taken from her."

The gospel of the Lord.

25. THE BLESSED VIRGIN MARY, IMAGE AND MOTHER OF THE CHURCH

I

FIRST READING

I will put enmity between your offspring and her offspring.

A reading from the book of Genesis   3:9-15, 20

A fter the man and woman had eaten of the tree,
the LORD God called to the man and asked him,
"Where are you?"
The man answered, "I heard you in the garden;
but I was afraid, because I was naked,
so I hid myself."
Then the LORD God asked, "Who told you that you were
naked?
You have eaten, then,
from the tree of which I had forbidden you to eat!"
The man replied, "The woman whom you put here with
me—
she gave me fruit from the tree, and so I ate it."
The LORD God then asked the woman,
"Why did you do such a thing?"
The woman answered, "The serpent tricked me into it, so I
ate it."

Then the LORD God said to the serpent:
"Because you have done this, you shall be banned
from all the animals
and from all the wild creatures;
on your belly shall you crawl,
and dirt shall you eat
all the days of your life.
I will put enmity between you and the woman,
and between your offspring and hers;
her offspring will strike at your head,
while you strike at their heel."

The man called his wife Eve,
because she became the mother of all the living.

The word of the Lord.

118

RESPONSORIAL PSALM   Judith 13:18bcde, 19

℟. (15:9d) You are the highest honor of our race.

**Blessed are you, daughter, by the Most High God,
above all women on earth;
and blessed be the LORD God,
the creator of heaven and earth.**

℟. You are the highest honor of our race.

**Your deed of hope will never be forgotten
by those who tell of the might of God.**

℟. You are the highest honor of our race.

ALLELUIA

℟. Alleluia, alleluia.

**Happy are you, holy Virgin Mary, deserving of all praise;
from you rose the sun of justice, Christ the Lord.**

℟. Alleluia, alleluia.

GOSPEL

Woman, this is your son. This is your mother.

✠ A reading from the holy gospel according to John   19:25-27

Standing by the cross of Jesus were his mother
and his mother's sister, Mary the wife of Clopas,
and Mary of Magdala.
**When Jesus saw his mother and the disciple whom he loved
standing beside her,
he said to his mother, "Woman, behold, your son."
Then he said to the disciple,
"Behold, your mother."
And from that hour the disciple took her into his home.**

The gospel of the Lord.

26. THE BLESSED VIRGIN MARY, IMAGE AND MOTHER OF THE CHURCH

II

FIRST READING

With one heart the disciples continued in steadfast prayer with Mary, the mother of Jesus.

A reading from the Acts of the Apostles 1:12-14

After Jesus had been taken up into heaven,
   the apostles returned to Jerusalem
   from the mount called Olivet, which is near Jerusalem,
   a sabbath day's journey away.

When the apostles entered the city
   they went to the upper room where they were staying,
   Peter and John and James and Andrew,
   Philip and Thomas, Bartholomew and Matthew,
   James son of Alphaeus, Simon the Zealot,
   and Judas son of James.
All these devoted themselves with one accord to prayer,
   together with some women,
   and Mary the mother of Jesus, and his brothers.

The word of the Lord.

RESPONSORIAL PSALM Psalm 87:1-2, 3 and 5, 6-7

℞. (3) Glorious things are told of you, O city of God.

The LORD loves the city
founded on holy mountains,
loves the gates of Zion
more than any dwelling in Jacob.

℞. Glorious things are told of you, O city of God.

Glorious things are said of you,
O city of God!
But of Zion it must be said:
"They all were born right here."

℞. Glorious things are told of you, O city of God.

The Most High confirms this;
the LORD notes in the register of the peoples:
"This one was born here."
So all sing in their festive dance:
"Within you is my true home."

℟. Glorious things are told of you, O city of God.

ALLELUIA

℟. Alleluia, alleluia.

O happy Virgin, you gave birth to the Lord;
O blessed mother of the Church,
you warm our hearts with the Spirit of your Son
    Jesus Christ.

℟. Alleluia, alleluia.

GOSPEL

The mother of Jesus was there. And his disciples believed in him.

✠ A reading from the holy gospel according to John   2:1-11

There was a wedding in Cana in Galilee,
    and the mother of Jesus was there.
Jesus and his disciples were also invited to the wedding.
When the wine ran short,
    the mother of Jesus said to him,
    "They have no wine."
And Jesus said to her,
    "Woman, how does your concern affect me?
My hour has not yet come."
His mother said to the servers,
    "Do whatever he tells you."
Now there were six stone water jars there for Jewish cere-
    monial washings,
    each holding twenty to thirty gallons.

Jesus told the servers,
>   "Fill the jars with water."
So they filled them to the brim.
Then Jesus told them,
>   "Draw some out now and take it to the headwaiter."
So they took it.
And when the headwaiter tasted the water that had become
>   wine,
>   without knowing where it came from
>   (although the servers who had drawn the water knew),
>   the headwaiter called the bridegroom and said to him,
>   "Everyone serves good wine first,
>   and then when people have drunk freely, an inferior
>   one;
>   but you have kept the good wine until now."
Jesus did this as the beginning of his signs in Cana in
>   Galilee
>   and so revealed his glory,
>   and his disciples began to believe in him.

The gospel of the Lord.

27. THE BLESSED VIRGIN MARY, IMAGE AND MOTHER OF THE CHURCH

III

FIRST READING

I saw the new Jerusalem, as beautiful as a bride all dressed for her husband.

A reading from the book of Revelation   21:1-5a

I, John, saw a new heaven and a new earth.
  The former heaven and the former earth had passed
    away,
  and the sea was no more.
I also saw the holy city, a new Jerusalem,
  coming down out of heaven from God,
  prepared as a bride adorned for her husband.
I heard a loud voice from the throne saying,
  "Behold, God's dwelling is with the human race.
God will dwell with them and they will be his people
  and God himself will always be with them as their God.
God will wipe every tear from their eyes,
  and there shall be no more death or mourning, wailing
    or pain,
  for the old order has passed away."

The One who sat on the throne said,
  "Behold, I make all things new."

                            The word of the Lord.

RESPONSORIAL PSALM   Isaiah 12:2-3, 4bcd, 5-6

    ℟. (6b) Among you is the great and Holy One of Israel.

God indeed is my savior;
I am confident and unafraid.
My strength and my courage is the LORD,
and he has been my savior.
With joy you will draw water
at the fountain of salvation.

    ℟. Among you is the great and Holy One of Israel.

Give thanks to the LORD, acclaim his name;
among the nations make known his deeds,
proclaim how exalted is his name.

R̷. Among you is the great and Holy One of Israel.

Sing praise to the LORD for his glorious achievement;
let this be known throughout all the earth.
Shout with exultation, O city of Zion,
for great in your midst
is the Holy One of Israel!

R̷. Among you is the great and Holy One of Israel.

ALLELUIA
See Luke 1:28

R̷. Alleluia, alleluia.

Hail, Mary, full of grace, the Lord is with you;
blessed are you among women.

R̷. Alleluia, alleluia.

GOSPEL

He will rule over the house of Jacob for ever.

✠ A reading from the holy gospel according to Luke   1:26-38

The angel Gabriel was sent from God
    to a town of Galilee called Nazareth,
    to a virgin betrothed to a man named Joseph,
    of the house of David,
    and the virgin's name was Mary.
And coming to Mary, the angel said,
    "Hail, favored one! The Lord is with you."
But Mary was greatly troubled at what was said
    and pondered what sort of greeting this might be.
Then the angel said to her,
    "Do not be afraid, Mary,
    for you have found favor with God.

"Behold, you will conceive in your womb and bear a son,
   and you shall name him Jesus.
He will be great and will be called Son of the Most High,
   and the Lord God will give him the throne of David his
      father,
   and he will rule over the house of Jacob forever,
   and of his kingdom there will be no end."
But Mary said to the angel,
   "How can this be,
   since I have no relations with a man?"
And the angel said to her in reply,
   "The holy Spirit will come upon you,
   and the power of the Most High will overshadow you.
Therefore the child to be born
   will be called holy, the Son of God.
And behold, Elizabeth, your relative,
   has also conceived a son in her old age,
   and this is the sixth month for her who was called
      barren;
   for nothing will be impossible for God."
Mary said, "Behold, I am the handmaid of the Lord.
May it be done to me according to your word."
Then the angel departed from her.

                              The gospel of the Lord.

28. THE IMMACULATE HEART OF THE BLESSED VIRGIN MARY

FIRST READING

You are the highest honor of our race.

A reading from the book of Judith   13:17-20; 15:9

All the people were greatly astonished.
    They bowed down and worshiped God, saying with
        one accord,
    "Blessed are you, our God,
    who today have brought to naught the enemies of your
        people."
Then Uzziah said to her:
    "Blessed are you, daughter, by the Most High God,
    above all the women on earth;
    and blessed be the LORD God,
    the creator of heaven and earth,
    who guided your blow at the head of the chief of our
        enemies.
Your deed of hope will never be forgotten
    by those who tell of the might of God.
May God make this redound to your everlasting honor,
    rewarding you with blessings,
    because you risked your life
    when your people were being oppressed,
    and you averted our disaster,
    walking uprightly before our God."
And all the people answered, "Amen! Amen!"

When they had visited her, all with one accord blessed her,
        saying:
    "You are the glory of Jerusalem,
        the surpassing joy of Israel;
        you are the splendid boast of our people."

                                        The word of the Lord.

126

RESPONSORIAL PSALM   Luke 1:46-48a, 48b-49, 50-51, 52-53, 54-55

R̸. (49) The Almighty has done great things for me.

My soul proclaims the greatness of the Lord;
my spirit rejoices in God my savior.
For he has looked upon his handmaid's lowliness;

R̸. The Almighty has done great things for me.

Behold, from now on will all ages call me blessed.
The Mighty One has done great things for me,
and holy is his name.

R̸. The Almighty has done great things for me.

The Lord's mercy is from age to age
to those who fear him.
He has shown might with his arm,
dispersed the arrogant of mind and heart.

R̸. The Almighty has done great things for me.

He has thrown down the rulers from their thrones
but lifted up the lowly.
The hungry he has filled with good things;
the rich he has sent away empty.

R̸. The Almighty has done great things for me.

The Lord has helped Israel his servant,
remembering his mercy,
according to his promise to our ancestors,
to Abraham and to his descendants for ever.

R̸. The Almighty has done great things for me.

ALLELUIA

R̸. Alleluia, alleluia.

Blessed are you, O Virgin Mary,
who bore the Son of the eternal Father.

R̸. Alleluia, alleluia.

GOSPEL

A   Blessed is the womb that bore you.

✠ A reading from the holy gospel according to Luke   11:27-28

While Jesus was speaking,
   a woman from the crowd called out and said to him,
   "Blessed is the womb that carried you
   and the breasts at which you nursed."
He replied,
   "Rather, blessed are those
   who hear the word of God and observe it."

The gospel of the Lord.

B   The mother of Jesus treasured all these things in her heart.

✠ A reading from the holy gospel according to Luke   2:46-51

After three days Jesus' parents found him in the temple,
   sitting in the midst of the teachers,
   listening to them and asking them questions,
   and all who heard him were astounded
   at his understanding and his answers.
When Jesus' parents saw him,
   they were astonished,
   and his mother said to him,
   "Son, why have you done this to us?
Your father and I have been looking for you with great
      anxiety."
And Jesus said to them,
   "Why were you looking for me?
Did you not know that I must be in my Father's house?"
But his parents did not understand what he said to them.
Jesus went down with them and came to Nazareth,
   and was obedient to them;
   and his mother kept all these things in her heart.

The gospel of the Lord.

29. THE BLESSED VIRGIN MARY, QUEEN OF ALL CREATION

FIRST READING

A

The dominion of the Lord is boundless.

✠ A reading from the book of the prophet Isaiah   9:1-3, 5-6

The people who walked in darkness
  have seen a great light;
upon those who dwelt in the land of gloom
  a light has shone.
You have brought them abundant joy
  and great rejoicing,
as they rejoice before you as at the harvest,
  as people make merry when dividing spoils.
For the yoke that burdened them,
  the pole on their shoulder,
and the rod of their taskmaster
  you have smashed, as on the day of Midian.
For a child is born to us, a son is given us;
  upon his shoulder dominion rests.
They name him Wonder-Counselor, God-Hero,
  Father-Forever, Prince of Peace.
His dominion is vast
  and forever peaceful,
from David's throne, and over his kingdom,
  which he confirms and sustains
by judgment and justice,
  both now and forever.
The zeal of the LORD of hosts will do this!

The word of the Lord.

B

Or reading no. I, 8 or no. II, 12 in the Appendix, page 213 or 220.

RESPONSORIAL PSALM   Psalm 45:11-12, 14-15, 16-17, 18

℟. (11a) Listen to me, daughter; see and bend your ear.

Listen, my daughter, and understand;
pay me careful heed.

129

Forget your people and your father's house,
that the king might desire your beauty.

R̷. Listen to me, daughter; see and bend your ear.

All glorious is the king's daughter as she enters,
her raiment threaded with gold;
in embroidered apparel she is led to the king.
The maids of her train are presented to the king.

R̷. Listen to me, daughter; see and bend your ear.

They are led in with glad and joyous acclaim;
they enter the palace of the king.
The throne of your fathers your sons will have;
you shall make them princes through all the land.

R̷. Listen to me, daughter; see and bend your ear.

I will make your name renowned through all generations;
thus nations shall praise you forever.

R̷. Listen to me, daughter; see and bend your ear.

ALLELUIA   See Luke 1:28

R̷. Alleluia, alleluia.

Hail, Mary, full of grace, the Lord is with you;
blessed are you among women.

R̷. Alleluia, alleluia.

GOSPEL

You will conceive and bear a son.

✠ A reading from the holy gospel according to Luke   1:26-38

The angel Gabriel was sent from God
    to a town of Galilee called Nazareth,
    to a virgin betrothed to a man named Joseph,
    of the house of David,
    and the virgin's name was Mary.
And coming to Mary, the angel said,
    "Hail, favored one! The Lord is with you."
But Mary was greatly troubled at what was said
    and pondered what sort of greeting this might be.

Then the angel said to her,
    "Do not be afraid, Mary,
    for you have found favor with God.

"Behold, you will conceive in your womb and bear a son,
    and you shall name him Jesus.
He will be great and will be called Son of the Most High,
    and the Lord God will give him the throne of David his
        father,
    and he will rule over the house of Jacob forever,
    and of his kingdom there will be no end."
But Mary said to the angel,
    "How can this be,
    since I have no relations with a man?"
And the angel said to her in reply,
    "The holy Spirit will come upon you,
    and the power of the Most High will overshadow you.
Therefore the child to be born
    will be called holy, the Son of God.
And behold, Elizabeth, your relative,
    has also conceived a son in her old age,
    and this is the sixth month for her who was called
        barren;
    for nothing will be impossible for God."
Mary said, "Behold, I am the handmaid of the Lord.
May it be done to me according to your word."
Then the angel departed from her.

                                    The gospel of the Lord.

SECTION 2

This section contains nine Mass formularies for the celebration of a memorial of the Mother of the Lord under titles that refer to her co-operation in fostering the spiritual life of the faithful.

MASS FORMULARIES

30. The Blessed Virgin Mary, Mother and Mediatrix of Grace
31. The Blessed Virgin Mary, Fountain of Salvation, I, II
32. The Blessed Virgin Mary, Mother and Teacher in the Spirit
33. The Blessed Virgin Mary, Mother of Good Counsel
34. The Blessed Virgin Mary, Cause of Our Joy
35. The Blessed Virgin Mary, Pillar of Faith
36. The Blessed Virgin Mary, Mother of Fairest Love
37. The Blessed Virgin Mary, Mother of Divine Hope
38. Holy Mary, Mother of Unity

30. THE BLESSED VIRGIN MARY, MOTHER AND MEDIATRIX OF GRACE

FIRST READING

How can I bear to see the evil that is to befall my people?

A reading from the book of Esther   8:3-8, 16-17a

In another audience with the king, Esther fell at his feet
    and tearfully implored him to revoke the harm done by
        Haman the Agagite,
and the plan he had devised against the Jews.

The king stretched forth the golden scepter to Esther.
So she rose and, standing in his presence, said:
    "If it pleases your majesty and seems proper to you,
    and if I have found favor with you and you love me,
    let a document be issued to revoke the letters
    which that schemer Haman, son of Hammedatha the
        Agagite,
    wrote for the destruction of the Jews in all the royal
        provinces.
For how can I witness the evil that is to befall my people,
    and how can I behold the destruction of my race?"

King Ahasuerus then said to Queen Esther and to the Jew
        Mordecai:
"Now that I have given Esther the house of Haman,
    and they have hanged him on the gibbet because he
        attacked the Jews,
    you in turn may write in the king's name what you see
        fit concerning the Jews
    and seal the letter with the royal signet ring."
For whatever is written in the name of the king
    and sealed with the royal signet ring cannot be revoked.

And there was splendor and merriment for the Jews,
    exultation and triumph.
In each and every province and in each and every city,
    wherever the king's order arrived,
    there was merriment and exultation,
    banqueting and feasting for the Jews.
And many of the peoples of the land embraced Judaism.

The word of the Lord.

RESPONSORIAL PSALM   Psalm 67:2-3, 4-5, 6-7

℟. (see 2b) Make your face shine upon us, O God.

May God be gracious to us and bless us;
may God's face shine upon us.
So shall your rule be known upon the earth,
your saving power among all the nations.

℟. Make your face shine upon us, O God.

May the peoples praise you, God;
may all the peoples praise you!
May the nations be glad and shout for joy;
for you govern the peoples justly,
you guide the nations upon the earth.

℟. Make your face shine upon us, O God.

May the peoples praise you, God;
may all the peoples praise you!
The earth has yielded its harvest;
God, our God, blesses us.

℟. Make your face shine upon us, O God.

ALLELUIA

℟. Alleluia, alleluia.

Happy are you, holy Virgin Mary,
queen of mercy and mother of grace;
from you arose our mediator and Savior, Christ the
Lord.

℟. Alleluia, alleluia.

GOSPEL

The mother of Jesus said to him: They have no wine.

✠ **A reading from the holy gospel according to John**   2:1-11

There was a wedding in Cana in Galilee,
  and the mother of Jesus was there.
Jesus and his disciples were also invited to the wedding.
When the wine ran short,
    the mother of Jesus said to him,
    "They have no wine."

And Jesus said to her,
    "Woman, how does your concern affect me?
My hour has not yet come."
His mother said to the servers,
    "Do whatever he tells you."
Now there were six stone water jars there for Jewish cere-
        monial washings,
    each holding twenty to thirty gallons.
Jesus told the servers,
    "Fill the jars with water."
So they filled them to the brim.
Then Jesus told them,
    "Draw some out now and take it to the headwaiter."
So they took it.
And when the headwaiter tasted the water that had become
        wine,
    without knowing where it came from
    (although the servers who had drawn the water knew),
    the headwaiter called the bridegroom and said to him,
    "Everyone serves good wine first,
    and then when people have drunk freely, an inferior
        one;
    but you have kept the good wine until now."
Jesus did this as the beginning of his signs in Cana in
        Galilee
    and so revealed his glory,
    and his disciples began to believe in him.

                          The gospel of the Lord.

31. THE BLESSED VIRGIN MARY, FOUNTAIN OF SALVATION

I

FIRST READING

I saw water flowing from the temple, and all who were touched by it were saved.

A reading from the book of the prophet Ezekiel   47:1-2, 8-9, 12

The angel brought me, Ezekiel,
      back to the entrance of the temple of the LORD,
      and I saw water flowing out
      from beneath the threshold of the temple toward the
            east,
      for the facade of the temple was toward the east;
      the water flowed down from the southern side of the
            temple,
      south of the altar.
The angel led me outside by the north gate,
      and around to the outer gate facing the east,
      where I saw water trickling from the southern side.
The angel said to me,
      "This water flows into the eastern district down upon
            the Arabah,
      and empties into the sea, the salt waters, which it makes
            fresh.
Wherever the river flows,
      every sort of living creature that can multiply shall live,
      and there shall be abundant fish,
      for wherever this water comes the sea shall be made
            fresh.
Along both banks of the river, fruit trees of every kind shall
            grow;
      their leaves shall not fade, nor their fruit fail.
Every month they shall bear fresh fruit,
      for they shall be watered by the flow from the
            sanctuary.
Their fruit shall serve for food, and their leaves for
            medicine."

The word of the Lord.

136

RESPONSORIAL PSALM   Isaiah 12:2-3, 4bcd, 5-6

℟. (3) You will draw water joyfully from the springs of salvation.

God indeed is my savior;
I am confident and unafraid.
My strength and my courage is the Lord,
and he has been my savior.
With joy you will draw water
at the fountain of salvation.

℟. You will draw water joyfully from the springs of salvation.

Give thanks to the Lord, acclaim his name;
among the nations make known his deeds,
proclaim how exalted is his name.

℟. You will draw water joyfully from the springs of salvation.

Sing praise to the Lord for his glorious achievement;
let this be known throughout all the earth.
Shout with exultation, O city of Zion,
for great in your midst
is the Holy One of Israel!

℟. You will draw water joyfully from the springs of salvation.

ALLELUIA

℟. Alleluia, alleluia.

Blessed are you among women,
for you gave birth to Christ, the Son of God
and Redeemer of us all.

℟. Alleluia, alleluia.

GOSPEL

One of the soldiers pierced his side with a lance, and immediately there came out blood and water.

✠ A reading from the holy gospel according to John   19:25-37

Standing by the cross of Jesus were his mother
    and his mother's sister, Mary the wife of Clopas,
    and Mary of Magdala.
When Jesus saw his mother and the disciple whom he loved
        standing beside her,
    he said to his mother, "Woman, behold, your son."
Then he said to the disciple,
    "Behold, your mother."
And from that hour the disciple took her into his home.

After this, aware that everything was now finished,
    in order that the scripture might be fulfilled,
    Jesus said, "I thirst."
There was a vessel filled with common wine.
So they put a sponge soaked in wine on a sprig of hyssop
    and put it up to his mouth.
When Jesus had taken the wine, he said,
    "It is finished."
And bowing his head, he handed over the spirit.

Now since it was preparation day,
    in order that the bodies might not remain on the cross
        on the sabbath,
    for the sabbath day of that week was a solemn one,
    the leaders of the Jews asked Pilate that their legs be
        broken
    and the bodies be taken down.
So the soldiers came and broke the legs of the first
    and then of the other one who was crucified with Jesus.
But when they came to Jesus and saw that he was already
        dead,
    they did not break his legs,
    but one soldier thrust his lance into his side,
    and immediately blood and water flowed out.

An eyewitness has testified, and his testimony is true;
he knows that he is speaking the truth,
so that you also may come to believe.
For this happened so that the scripture passage might be
fulfilled:
"Not a bone of it will be broken."
And again another passage says:
"They will look upon him whom they have pierced."

The gospel of the Lord.

II

FIRST READING

Fountain of the garden, well of living water.

✛ **A reading from the Song of Songs**   4:6-7, 9, 12-15

Until the day breathes cool and the shadows lengthen,
 I will go to the mountain of myrrh,
  to the hill of incense.
You are all-beautiful, my beloved,
  and there is no blemish in you.

You have ravished my heart, my sister, my bride;
  you have ravished my heart with one glance of your
   eyes,
  with one bead of your necklace.

You are an enclosed garden, my sister, my bride,
  an enclosed garden, a fountain sealed.
You are a park that puts forth pomegranates,
  with all choice fruits;
nard and saffron, calamus and cinnamon,
  with all kinds of incense;
myrrh and aloes,
  with all the finest spices.
You are a garden fountain, a well of water
  flowing fresh from Lebanon.

The word of the Lord.

RESPONSORIAL PSALM   Judith 13:18bcde, 19

℟. (15:9d) You are the highest honor of our race.

Blessed are you, daughter, by the Most High God,
above all women on earth;
and blessed be the LORD God,
the creator of heaven and earth.

℟. You are the highest honor of our race.

Your deed of hope will never be forgotten
by those who tell of the might of God.

℟. You are the highest honor of our race.

ALLELUIA   See Luke 1:45, 49

℟. Alleluia, alleluia.

Blessed are you, O Virgin Mary, for firmly believing that the Almighty has done great things for you.

℟. Alleluia, alleluia.

GOSPEL

Streams of living water shall flow from his heart.

✠ **A reading from the holy gospel according to John**   7:37-39a

On the last and greatest day of the feast,
Jesus stood up and exclaimed,
   "Let anyone who thirsts come to me and drink.
Whoever believes in me, as scripture says:
   Rivers of living water will flow from within him."
Jesus said this in reference to the Spirit
   that those who came to believe in him were to receive.

The gospel of the Lord.

32. THE BLESSED VIRGIN MARY, MOTHER AND TEACHER IN THE SPIRIT

FIRST READING

A   Whoever finds me, finds life.

A reading from the book of Proverbs   8:17-21, 34-35

Wisdom says:
   "Those who love me, I also love,
      and those who seek me find me.
With me are riches and honor,
      enduring wealth and prosperity.
My fruit is better than gold,
      yes, than pure gold,
      and my revenue than choice silver.
On the way of duty I walk,
      along the paths of justice,
granting wealth to those who love me,
      and filling their treasuries.

"Happy the person watching daily at my gates,
      waiting at my doorposts;
for the one who finds me finds life,
      and wins favor from the LORD."

The word of the Lord.

B   My house will be called a house of prayer for all the peoples.

A reading from the book of the prophet Isaiah   56:1, 6-7

Thus says the LORD:
   Observe what is right, do what is just;
      for my salvation is about to come,
      my justice, about to be revealed.

The foreigners who join themselves to the LORD,
      ministering to him,
loving the name of the LORD,
      and becoming his servants—
all who keep the sabbath free from profanation
      and hold to my covenant,

them I will bring to my holy mountain
  and make joyful in my house of prayer;
their holocausts and sacrifices
  will be acceptable on my altar,
for my house shall be called
  a house of prayer for all peoples.

The word of the Lord.

RESPONSORIAL PSALM   Psalm 15:2-3a, 3bc-4, 5

℟. (see 1b) The just shall live on your holy mountain, O
    Lord.

Whoever walks without blame,
doing what is right,
speaking truth from the heart;
who does not slander a neighbor.

℟. The just shall live on your holy mountain, O Lord.

Who does no harm to another,
never defames a friend;
who disdains the wicked,
but honors those who fear the LORD.

℟. The just shall live on your holy mountain, O Lord.

Who keeps an oath despite the cost,
lends no money at interest,
accepts no bribe against the innocent.
Whoever acts like this
shall never be shaken.

℟. The just shall live on your holy mountain, O Lord.

ALLELUIA   See Luke 2:19

℟. Alleluia, alleluia.

**Blessed is the Virgin Mary who kept the word of God
and pondered it in her heart.**

℟. Alleluia, alleluia.

GOSPEL

A   Extending his hands toward the disciples, he said: Here are my mother and my brothers.

✠ **A reading from the holy gospel according to Matthew**

12:46-50

While Jesus was speaking to the crowds,
  his mother and his brothers appeared outside,
  wishing to speak with him.
Someone told him, "Your mother and your brothers are
      standing outside,
  asking to speak with you."
But Jesus said in reply to the one who told him,
  "Who is my mother? Who are my brothers?"
And stretching out his hand toward his disciples, he said,
  "Here are my mother and my brothers.
For whoever does the will of my heavenly Father
  is my brother, and sister, and mother."

The gospel of the Lord.

B   Woman, this is your son. This is your mother.

✠ **A reading from the holy gospel according to John**   19:25-27

Standing by the cross of Jesus were his mother
  and his mother's sister, Mary the wife of Clopas,
  and Mary of Magdala.
When Jesus saw his mother and the disciple whom he loved
      standing beside her,
  he said to his mother, "Woman, behold, your son."
Then he said to the disciple,
  "Behold, your mother."
And from that hour the disciple took her into his home.

The gospel of the Lord.

C   Or reading no. III, 19 in the Appendix, page 231.

33. THE BLESSED VIRGIN MARY, MOTHER OF GOOD COUNSEL

FIRST READING

A   The Wonderful Counselor is given to us.

A reading from the book of the prophet Isaiah   9:1-3, 5-6

The people who walked in darkness
    have seen a great light;
upon those who dwelt in the land of gloom
    a light has shone.
You have brought them abundant joy
    and great rejoicing,
as they rejoice before you as at the harvest,
    as people make merry when dividing spoils.
For the yoke that burdened them,
    the pole on their shoulder,
and the rod of their taskmaster
    you have smashed, as on the day of Midian.
For a child is born to us, a son is given us;
    upon his shoulder dominion rests.
They name him Wonder-Counselor, God-Hero,
    Father-Forever, Prince of Peace.
His dominion is vast
    and forever peaceful,
from David's throne, and over his kingdom,
    which he confirms and sustains
by judgment and justice,
    both now and forever.
The zeal of the LORD of hosts will do this!

The word of the Lord.

B With one heart the disciples continued in steadfast prayer with Mary, the mother of Jesus.

A reading from the Acts of the Apostles
1:12-14; 2:1-4

After Jesus had been taken up into heaven,
  the apostles returned to Jerusalem
from the mount called Olivet, which is near Jerusalem,
a sabbath day's journey away.

When the apostles entered the city
  they went to the upper room where they were staying,
  Peter and John and James and Andrew,
  Philip and Thomas, Bartholomew and Matthew,
  James son of Alphaeus, Simon the Zealot,
  and Judas son of James.
All these devoted themselves with one accord to prayer,
  together with some women,
  and Mary the mother of Jesus, and his brothers.

When the time for Pentecost was fulfilled,
  the apostles were all in one place together.
And suddenly there came from the sky
  a noise like a strong driving wind,
  and it filled the entire house in which they were.
Then there appeared to them tongues as of fire,
  which parted and came to rest on each one of them.
And they were all filled with the holy Spirit
  and began to speak in different tongues,
  as the Spirit enabled them to proclaim.

The word of the Lord.

RESPONSORIAL PSALM
Sirach 14:20, 21-22, 23-25, 26-27

℟. (20a) Blessed are those who meditate on wisdom.

Happy those who meditate on wisdom,
and reflect on knowledge.

℟. Blessed are those who meditate on wisdom.

Who ponder her ways in their hearts,
and understand her paths.

℟. Blessed are those who meditate on wisdom.

**Who peep through her windows,
and listen at her doors;
who encamp near her house,
and fasten their tent pegs next to her walls;
who pitch their tents beside her,
and live as her welcome neighbors.**

℟. Blessed are those who meditate on wisdom.

**Who build their nests in her leafage,
and lodge in her branches;
who take shelter with her from the heat,
and dwell in her home.**

℟. Blessed are those who meditate on wisdom.

ALLELUIA   Proverbs 8:14

℟. Alleluia, alleluia.

**To me belong counsel and prudence;
understanding and strength are mine.**

℟. Alleluia, alleluia.

GOSPEL

The mother of Jesus said to the attendants: Do whatever he tells you.

✠ **A reading from the holy gospel according to John**   2:1-11

There was a wedding in Cana in Galilee,
and the mother of Jesus was there.
**Jesus and his disciples were also invited to the wedding.
When the wine ran short,
the mother of Jesus said to him,
"They have no wine."
And Jesus said to her,
"Woman, how does your concern affect me?
My hour has not yet come."
His mother said to the servers,
"Do whatever he tells you."**

Now there were six stone water jars there for Jewish cere-
monial washings,
each holding twenty to thirty gallons.
Jesus told the servers,
"Fill the jars with water."
So they filled them to the brim.
Then Jesus told them,
"Draw some out now and take it to the headwaiter."
So they took it.
And when the headwaiter tasted the water that had become
wine,
without knowing where it came from
(although the servers who had drawn the water knew),
the headwaiter called the bridegroom and said to him,
"Everyone serves good wine first,
and then when people have drunk freely, an inferior
one;
but you have kept the good wine until now."
Jesus did this as the beginning of his signs in Cana in
Galilee
and so revealed his glory,
and his disciples began to believe in him.

The gospel of the Lord.

34. THE BLESSED VIRGIN MARY, CAUSE OF OUR JOY

FIRST READING

A   Rejoice and be glad, Daughter of Zion.

A reading from the book of the prophet Zechariah   2:14-17

Sing and rejoice, O daughter Zion!
    See, I am coming to dwell among you, says the LORD.
Many nations shall join themselves to the LORD on that day,
      and they shall be his people,
      and he will dwell among you,
      and you shall know that the LORD of hosts has sent me
         to you.
The LORD will possess Judah as his portion in the holy land,
      and he will again choose Jerusalem.
Silence, all people, in the presence of the LORD!
      for the LORD stirs forth from his holy dwelling.

                              The word of the Lord.

B   I exult for joy in the Lord.

A reading from the book of the prophet Isaiah   61:9-11

The descendants of my people shall be renowned among
      the nations,
      and their offspring among the peoples;
all who see them shall acknowledge them
      as a race the LORD has blessed.

I rejoice heartily in the LORD,
      in my God is the joy of my soul;
for he has clothed me with a robe of salvation,
      and wrapped me in a mantle of justice,
like a bridegroom adorned with a diadem,
      like a bride bedecked with her jewels.
As the earth brings forth its plants,
      and a garden makes its growth spring up,
so will the Lord GOD make justice and praise
      spring up before all the nations.

                              The word of the Lord.

RESPONSORIAL PSALM   Luke 1:46-48, 49-50, 53-54

℟. (See Isaiah 61:10b) My spirit rejoices in my God.

My soul proclaims the greatness of the Lord;
my spirit rejoices in God my savior.
For he has looked upon his handmaid's lowliness;
behold, from now on will all ages call me blessed.

℟. My spirit rejoices in my God.

The Mighty One has done great things for me,
and holy is his name.
The Lord's mercy is from age to age
to those who fear him.

℟. My spirit rejoices in my God.

The hungry he has filled with good things;
the rich he has sent away empty.
The Lord has helped Israel his servant,
remembering his mercy.

℟. My spirit rejoices in my God.

ALLELUIA

℟. Alleluia, alleluia.

Hail, holy Mary, joy of humankind,
remaining a virgin, you gave birth
and brought forth for us
the One who is our salvation and joy.

℟. Alleluia, alleluia.

GOSPEL

A   As soon as Elizabeth heard Mary's greeting, the infant leaped in her womb.

✠ **A reading from the holy gospel according to Luke**   1:39-47

Mary set out
and traveled to the hill country in haste
to a town of Judah,
where she entered the house of Zechariah
and greeted Elizabeth.

When Elizabeth heard Mary's greeting,
    the infant leaped in her womb,
    and Elizabeth, filled with the holy Spirit,
    cried out in a loud voice and said,
    "Most blessed are you among women,
    and blessed is the fruit of your womb.
And how does this happen to me,
    that the mother of my Lord should come to me?
For at the moment the sound of your greeting reached my
        ears,
    the infant in my womb leaped for joy.
Blessed are you who believed
    that what was spoken to you by the Lord
    would be fulfilled."

And Mary said:
    "My soul proclaims the greatness of the Lord;
        my spirit rejoices in God my savior."

                    The gospel of the Lord.

B   May my joy be within you.

✠ A reading from the holy gospel according to John   15:9-12

Jesus said to his disciples:
    "As the Father loves me, so I also love you.
Remain in my love.
If you keep my commandments, you will remain in my love,
    just as I have kept my Father's commandments
    and remain in his love.

"I have told you this so that my joy may be in you
    and your joy may be complete.
This is my commandment: love one another as I love you."

                    The gospel of the Lord.

35. THE BLESSED VIRGIN MARY, PILLAR OF FAITH

FIRST READING

You have brought to nothing the enemies of your people.

A reading from the book of Judith   13:14, 17-20

Judith urged them with a loud voice:
"Praise God, praise God!
Praise God who has not withdrawn his mercy
from the house of Israel,
but has shattered our enemies by my hand this very
night."

All the people were greatly astonished.
They bowed down and worshiped God, saying with one
accord,
"Blessed are you, our God,
who today have brought to naught the enemies of your
people."
Then Uzziah said to her:
"Blessed are you, daughter, by the Most High God,
above all the women on earth;
and blessed be the Lord God,
the creator of heaven and earth,
who guided your blow at the head of the chief of our
enemies.
Your deed of hope will never be forgotten
by those who tell of the might of God.
May God make this redound to your everlasting honor,
rewarding you with blessings,
because you risked your life
when your people were being oppressed,
and you averted our disaster,
walking uprightly before our God."
And all the people answered, "Amen! Amen!"

The word of the Lord.

RESPONSORIAL PSALM   Psalm 27:1, 3, 4, 5

℟. (See 9cd) You are my help, my saving God.

The LORD is my light and my salvation;
whom do I fear?
The LORD is my life's refuge;
of whom am I afraid?

℟. You are my help, my saving God.

Though an army encamp against me,
my heart does not fear;
Though war be waged against me,
even then do I trust.

℟. You are my help, my saving God.

One thing I ask of the LORD;
this I seek:
To dwell in the LORD's house
all the days of my life,
To gaze on the LORD's beauty,
to visit the temple.

℟. You are my help, my saving God.

For God will hide me in this shelter
in time of trouble,
will conceal me in the cover of this tent;
and set me high upon a rock.

℟. You are my help, my saving God.

ALLELUIA   See Psalm 40:3-4

℟. Alleluia, alleluia.

God set my feet on rock
and put a new song in my mouth.

℟. Alleluia, alleluia.

GOSPEL

Blessed is the womb that bore you!

✠ **A reading from the holy gospel according to Luke**   11:27-28

While Jesus was speaking,
    a woman from the crowd called out and said to him,
    "Blessed is the womb that carried you
    and the breasts at which you nursed."
He replied,
    "Rather, blessed are those
    who hear the word of God and observe it."

The gospel of the Lord.

36. THE BLESSED VIRGIN MARY, MOTHER OF FAIREST LOVE

I am the mother of fairest love.

A reading from the book of Sirach   24:17-21

I bud forth delights like the vine,
　my blossoms become fruit fair and rich.
Come to me, all you that yearn for me,
　and be filled with my fruits.
You will remember me as sweeter than honey,
　better to have than the honeycomb.
Whoever eats of me will hunger still,
　whoever drinks of me will thirst for more;
whoever obeys me will not be put to shame,
　whoever serves me will never fail.

The word of the Lord.

RESPONSORIAL PSALM   Song of Songs 2:10bc and 14ef; 4:8a and 9a, 11cd and 12, 15

℟. (See 4:7) O Mary, you are all fair; there is no blemish
in you.

**Arise, my beloved, my beautiful one, and come!
For your voice is sweet,
and you are lovely.**

℟. O Mary, you are all fair; there is no blemish in you.

**Come from Lebanon, my bride,
you have ravished my heart, my sister, my bride.**

℟. O Mary, you are all fair; there is no blemish in you.

**And the fragrance of your garments
is the fragrance of Lebanon.
You are an enclosed garden, my sister, my bride,
an enclosed garden, a fountain sealed.**

℟. O Mary, you are all fair; there is no blemish in you.

**You are a garden fountain, a well of water
flowing fresh from Lebanon.**

℟. O Mary, you are all fair; there is no blemish in you.

ALLELUIA
See Luke 1:28

℟. Alleluia, alleluia.

**Hail, Mary, full of grace, the Lord is with you;
blessed are you among women.**

℟. Alleluia, alleluia.

GOSPEL

Hail, full of grace.

✠ **A reading from the holy gospel according to Luke**   1:26-38

The angel Gabriel was sent from God
    to a town of Galilee called Nazareth,
    to a virgin betrothed to a man named Joseph,
    of the house of David,
    and the virgin's name was Mary.
And coming to Mary, the angel said,
    "Hail, favored one! The Lord is with you."
But Mary was greatly troubled at what was said
    and pondered what sort of greeting this might be.
Then the angel said to her,
    "Do not be afraid, Mary,
    for you have found favor with God.

"Behold, you will conceive in your womb and bear a son,
    and you shall name him Jesus.
He will be great and will be called Son of the Most High,
    and the Lord God will give him the throne of David his
        father,
    and he will rule over the house of Jacob forever,
    and of his kingdom there will be no end."
But Mary said to the angel,
    "How can this be,
    since I have no relations with a man?"
And the angel said to her in reply,
    "The holy Spirit will come upon you,
    and the power of the Most High will overshadow you.
Therefore the child to be born
    will be called holy, the Son of God.

And behold, Elizabeth, your relative,
> has also conceived a son in her old age,
> and this is the sixth month for her who was called barren;
> for nothing will be impossible for God."

Mary said, "Behold, I am the handmaid of the Lord.
May it be done to me according to your word."
Then the angel departed from her.

The gospel of the Lord.

37. THE BLESSED VIRGIN MARY, MOTHER OF DIVINE HOPE

FIRST READING

I am the mother of divine hope.

A reading from the book of Sirach 24:9-12, 18-21

Before all ages, in the beginning, God created me,
    and through all ages I shall not cease to be.
In the holy tent I ministered before him,
    and in Zion I fixed my abode.
Thus in the chosen city God has given me rest,
    in Jerusalem is my domain.
I have struck root among the glorious people,
    in the portion of the Lord, his heritage.

Come to me, all you that yearn for me,
    and be filled with my fruits.
You will remember me as sweeter than honey,
    better to have than the honeycomb.
Whoever eats of me will hunger still,
    whoever drinks of me will thirst for more;
whoever obeys me will not be put to shame,
    whoever serves me will never fail.

The word of the Lord.

RESPONSORIAL PSALM Luke 1:46-48a, 48b-49, 50-51, 52-53, 54-55

℟. Hail, Virgin Mary, hope of God's people.

My soul proclaims the greatness of the Lord;
my spirit rejoices in God my savior.
For he has looked upon his handmaid's lowliness;

℟. Hail, Virgin Mary, hope of God's people.

Behold, from now on will all ages call me blessed.
The Mighty One has done great things for me,
and holy is his name.

℟. Hail, Virgin Mary, hope of God's people.

The Lord's mercy is from age to age
to those who fear him.
He has shown might with his arm,
dispersed the arrogant of mind and heart.

℟. Hail, Virgin Mary, hope of God's people.

He has thrown down the rulers from their thrones
but lifted up the lowly.
The hungry he has filled with good things;
the rich he has sent away empty.

℟. Hail, Virgin Mary, hope of God's people.

The Lord has helped Israel his servant,
remembering his mercy,
according to his promise to our ancestors,
to Abraham and to his descendants for ever.

℟. Hail, Virgin Mary, hope of God's people.

ALLELUIA

℟. Alleluia, alleluia.

Mother and Virgin and Queen of the world,
pray for your children to God who chose you.

℟. Alleluia, alleluia.

GOSPEL

The mother of Jesus was at the wedding feast with him.

✠ A reading from the holy gospel according to John   2:1-11

There was a wedding in Cana in Galilee,
   and the mother of Jesus was there.
Jesus and his disciples were also invited to the wedding.
When the wine ran short,
   the mother of Jesus said to him,
   "They have no wine."
And Jesus said to her,
   "Woman, how does your concern affect me?
My hour has not yet come."

His mother said to the servers,
  "Do whatever he tells you."
Now there were six stone water jars there for Jewish cere-
      monial washings,
  each holding twenty to thirty gallons.
Jesus told the servers,
  "Fill the jars with water."
So they filled them to the brim.
Then Jesus told them,
  "Draw some out now and take it to the headwaiter."
So they took it.
And when the headwaiter tasted the water that had become
      wine,
  without knowing where it came from
  (although the servers who had drawn the water knew),
  the headwaiter called the bridegroom and said to him,
  "Everyone serves good wine first,
  and then when people have drunk freely, an inferior
      one;
  but you have kept the good wine until now."
Jesus did this as the beginning of his signs in Cana in
      Galilee
  and so revealed his glory,
  and his disciples began to believe in him.

                                   The gospel of the Lord.

38. HOLY MARY, MOTHER OF UNITY

FIRST READING

A At the proper time I will gather you together.

A reading from the book of the prophet Zephaniah 3:14-20

Shout for joy, O daughter Zion!
    Sing joyfully, O Israel!
Be glad and exult with all your heart,
    O daughter Jerusalem!
The LORD has removed the judgment against you
    and turned away your enemies;
the King of Israel, the LORD, is in your midst,
    you have no further misfortune to fear.
On that day, it shall be said to Jerusalem:
    Fear not, O Zion, be not discouraged!
The LORD, your God, is in your midst,
    a mighty savior;
the LORD will rejoice over you with gladness,
    and renew you in his love,
the LORD will sing joyfully because of you,
    as one sings at festivals.

I will remove disaster from among you,
    so that none may recount your disgrace.
Yes, at that time I will deal
    with all who oppress you:
I will save the lame,
    and assemble the outcasts;
I will give them praise and renown
    in all the earth, when I bring about their restoration.
At that time I will bring you home,
    and at that time I will gather you;
for I will give you renown and praise,
    among all the peoples of the earth,
when I bring about your restoration
    before your very eyes, says the LORD.

The word of the Lord.

B   There is one mediator between God and humanity, Christ Jesus, himself human.

A reading from the first letter of Paul to Timothy   2:5-8

There is one God.
  There is also one mediator between God
  and the human race,
  Christ Jesus, himself human,
  who gave himself as ransom for all.
This was the testimony at the proper time.
For this I was appointed preacher and apostle
  (I am speaking the truth, I am not lying),
  teacher of the Gentiles in faith and truth.

It is my wish, then, that in every place you should pray,
  lifting up holy hands, without anger or argument.

The word of the Lord.

RESPONSORIAL PSALM   Jeremiah 31:10, 11-12ab, 13-14

R̸. (See 10c) Gather your scattered people, O Lord.

Hear the word of the LORD, O nations,
proclaim it on distant coasts, and say:
He who scattered Israel, now gathers them together,
he guards them as a shepherd his flock.

R̸. Gather your scattered people, O Lord.

The LORD shall ransom Jacob,
he shall redeem him from the hand of his conqueror.
Shouting, they shall mount the heights of Zion,
they shall come streaming to the LORD's blessings:
The grain, the wine, and the oil,
the sheep and the oxen.

R̸. Gather your scattered people, O Lord.

Then the virgins shall make merry and dance,
and young men and old as well.
I will turn their mourning into joy,
I will console and gladden them after their sorrows.
I will lavish choice portions upon the priests,
and my people shall be filled with my blessings.

R̸. Gather your scattered people, O Lord.

ALLELUIA

℟. Alleluia, alleluia.

**Let your Church be gathered, O Lord,
from the ends of the earth into your kingdom,
for glory and power are yours
through Jesus Christ for ever.**

℟. Alleluia, alleluia.

GOSPEL

A

He will gather together in unity the scattered children of God.

✠ **A reading from the holy gospel according to John**   11:45-52

Many of the Jewish people who had come to Mary and
Martha,
    the sisters of Lazarus,
    and had seen what Jesus had done began to believe in
        him.
But some of them went to the Pharisees
    and told them what Jesus had done.
So the chief priests and the Pharisees
    convened the Sanhedrin and said,
    "What are we going to do?
This man is performing many signs.
If we leave him alone, all will believe in him,
    and the Romans will come
    and take away both our land and our nation."
But one of them, Caiaphas,
    who was high priest that year, said to them,
    "You know nothing,
    nor do you consider that it is better for you
    that one man should die instead of the people,
    so that the whole nation may not perish."
Caiaphas did not say this on his own,
    but since he was high priest for that year,
    he prophesied that Jesus was going to die for the nation,
    and not only for the nation,
    but also to gather into one the dispersed children of God.**

The gospel of the Lord.

B   May they be completely one.

✠ **A reading from the holy gospel according to John**   17:20-26

Jesus raised his eyes to heaven and said:
  "I pray not only for my disciples,
    but also for those who will believe in me through their
      word,
    so that they may all be one,
    as you, Father, are in me and I in you,
    that they also may be in us,
    that the world may believe that you sent me.
And I have given them the glory you gave me,
    so that they may be one, as we are one,
    I in them and you in me,
    that they may be brought to perfection as one,
    that the world may know that you sent me,
    and that you loved them even as you loved me.
Father, they are your gift to me.
I wish that where I am they also may be with me,
    that they may see my glory that you gave me,
    because you loved me before the foundation of the
      world.
Righteous Father, the world also does not know you,
    but I know you, and they know that you sent me.
I made known to them your name and I will make it known,
    that the love with which you loved me
    may be in them and I in them."

                                The gospel of the Lord.

SECTION 3

This section contains eight Mass formularies for the celebration of a memorial of Mary under titles that refer to her merciful intercession on behalf of the faithful.

MASS FORMULARIES

39. Holy Mary, Queen and Mother of Mercy, I, II
40. The Blessed Virgin Mary, Mother of Divine Providence
41. The Blessed Virgin Mary, Mother of Consolation
42. The Blessed Virgin Mary, Help of Christians
43. Our Lady of Ransom
44. The Blessed Virgin Mary, Health of the Sick
45. The Blessed Virgin Mary, Queen of Peace
46. The Blessed Virgin Mary, Gate of Heaven

39. HOLY MARY, QUEEN AND MOTHER OF MERCY

I

FIRST READING

Queen Esther prays for her people.

A reading from the book of Esther C:12, 14-15, 25, 30

Queen Esther, seized with mortal anguish, had recourse
    to the LORD.
Then she prayed to the LORD, the God of Israel, saying:
"My LORD, our King, you alone are God.
Help me, who am alone and have no help but you,
    for I am taking my life in my hand.

"Save us by your power, and help me, who am alone
    and have no one but you, O LORD.

"O God, more powerful than all,
    hear the voice of those in despair.
Save us from the power of the wicked,
    and deliver me from my fear."

The word of the Lord.

RESPONSORIAL PSALM Luke 1:46-48a, 48b-49, 50-51, 52-53, 54-55

R̸. (See 50) The Lord has mercy in every generation.

**My soul proclaims the greatness of the Lord;
my spirit rejoices in God my savior.
For he has looked upon his handmaid's lowliness;**

R̸. The Lord has mercy in every generation.

**Behold, from now on will all ages call me blessed.
The Mighty One has done great things for me,
and holy is his name.**

R̸. The Lord has mercy in every generation.

**The Lord's mercy is from age to age
to those who fear him.
He has shown might with his arm,
dispersed the arrogant of mind and heart.**

R̸. The Lord has mercy in every generation.

He has thrown down the rulers from their thrones
but lifted up the lowly.
The hungry he has filled with good things;
the rich he has sent away empty.

℟. The Lord has mercy in every generation.

The Lord has helped Israel his servant,
remembering his mercy,
according to his promise to our ancestors,
to Abraham and to his descendants for ever.

℟. The Lord has mercy in every generation.

ALLELUIA

℟. Alleluia, alleluia.

Mary, Virgin for ever,
most worthy queen of the world,
pray for our peace and salvation,
for you are the mother of Christ,
the Lord and Savior of all.

℟. Alleluia, alleluia.

GOSPEL

The mother of Jesus was at the wedding feast with him.

✠ A reading from the holy gospel according to John   2:1-11

There was a wedding in Cana in Galilee,
  and the mother of Jesus was there.
Jesus and his disciples were also invited to the wedding.
When the wine ran short,
  the mother of Jesus said to him,
  "They have no wine."
And Jesus said to her,
  "Woman, how does your concern affect me?
My hour has not yet come."
His mother said to the servers,
  "Do whatever he tells you."
Now there were six stone water jars there for Jewish cere-
  monial washings,
  each holding twenty to thirty gallons.

Jesus told the servers,
   "Fill the jars with water."

So they filled them to the brim.
Then Jesus told them,
   "Draw some out now and take it to the headwaiter."
So they took it.
And when the headwaiter tasted the water that had become
         wine,
   without knowing where it came from
   (although the servers who had drawn the water knew),
   the headwaiter called the bridegroom and said to him,
   "Everyone serves good wine first,
   and then when people have drunk freely, an inferior
         one;
   but you have kept the good wine until now."
Jesus did this as the beginning of his signs in Cana in
         Galilee
   and so revealed his glory,
   and his disciples began to believe in him.

                              The gospel of the Lord.

II

FIRST READING

God is rich in mercy.

A reading from the letter of Paul to the Ephesians   2:4-10

Brothers and sisters:
**God, who is rich in mercy,
because of the great love he had for us,
even when we were dead in our transgressions,
brought us to life with Christ (by grace you have been
    saved),
raised us up with him,
and seated us with him in the heavens in Christ Jesus,
that in the ages to come
God might show the immeasurable riches of his grace
in his kindness to us in Christ Jesus.
For by grace you have been saved through faith,
and this is not from you; it is the gift of God;
it is not from works, so no one may boast.
For we are God's handiwork, created in Christ Jesus for
    good works
that God has prepared in advance,
that we should live in them.**

The word of the Lord.

RESPONSORIAL PSALM   Psalm 103:1-2, 3-4, 6 and 8, 13 and 17

℞. (See 17a) The Lord's kindness is everlasting.

**Bless the LORD, my soul;
all my being, bless his holy name!
Bless the LORD, my soul;
do not forget all the gifts of God.**

℞. The Lord's kindness is everlasting.

**Who pardons all your sins,
heals all your ills,
delivers your life from the pit,
surrounds you with love and compassion.**

℟. The Lord's kindness is everlasting.

The LORD does righteous deeds,
brings justice to all the oppressed.
Merciful and gracious is the LORD,
slow to anger, abounding in kindness.

℟. The Lord's kindness is everlasting.

As a father has compassion on his children,
so the LORD has compassion on the faithful.
But the LORD's kindness is forever
toward the faithful from age to age.

℟. The Lord's kindness is everlasting.

ALLELUIA

℟. Alleluia, alleluia.

Hail, Mother of the Lord, queen of mercy,
you are comfort for the world and hope for the down-
cast.

℟. Alleluia, alleluia.

GOSPEL

The Lord has mercy on those who fear him in every generation.

✛ **A reading from the holy gospel according to Luke** 1:39-55

Mary set out
and traveled to the hill country in haste
to a town of Judah,
where she entered the house of Zechariah
and greeted Elizabeth.
When Elizabeth heard Mary's greeting,
the infant leaped in her womb,
and Elizabeth, filled with the holy Spirit,
cried out in a loud voice and said,
"Most blessed are you among women,
and blessed is the fruit of your womb.
And how does this happen to me,
that the mother of my Lord should come to me?

For at the moment the sound of your greeting reached my
     ears,
     the infant in my womb leaped for joy.
Blessed are you who believed
     that what was spoken to you by the Lord
     would be fulfilled."

And Mary said:
     "My soul proclaims the greatness of the Lord;
          my spirit rejoices in God my savior.
     For he has looked upon his handmaid's lowliness;
          behold, from now on will all ages call me blessed.
     The Mighty One has done great things for me,
          and holy is his name.
     The Lord's mercy is from age to age
          to those who fear him.
     The Lord has shown might with his arm,
          dispersed the arrogant of mind and heart.
     The Lord has thrown down the rulers from their thrones
          but lifted up the lowly.
     The hungry he has filled with good things;
          the rich he has sent away empty.
     The Lord has helped Israel his servant,
          remembering his mercy,
     according to his promise to our ancestors,
          to Abraham and to his descendants forever."

                                   The gospel of the Lord.

40. THE BLESSED VIRGIN MARY, MOTHER OF DIVINE PROVIDENCE

FIRST READING

As a mother comforts her child, so I will comfort you.

A reading from the book of the prophet Isaiah   66:10-14

Rejoice with Jerusalem and be glad because of her,
    all you who love her;
exult, exult with her,
    all you who were mourning over her!
Oh, that you may suck fully
    of the milk of her comfort,
that you may nurse with delight
    at her abundant breasts!
        For thus says the LORD:
Lo, I will spread prosperity over Jerusalem like a river,
    and the wealth of the nations like an overflowing
        torrent.
As nurslings, you shall be carried in her arms,
    and fondled in her lap;
as a mother comforts her child,
    so will I comfort you;
    in Jerusalem you shall find your comfort.

When you see this, your heart shall rejoice,
    and your bodies flourish like the grass;
the LORD's power shall be known to his servants,
    but to his enemies his wrath.

                        The word of the Lord.

RESPONSORIAL PSALM   Psalm 131:1, 2, 3

    ℟. (See Psalm 57:2c) In you my soul takes refuge, O Lord.

LORD, my heart is not proud;
nor are my eyes haughty;
I do not busy myself with great matters,
with things too sublime for me.

    ℟. In you my soul takes refuge, O Lord.

172

Rather, I have stilled my soul,
hushed it like a weaned child.
Like a weaned child on its mother's lap,
so is my soul within me.

℟. In you my soul takes refuge, O Lord.

Israel, hope in the LORD,
now and forever.

℟. In you my soul takes refuge, O Lord.

ALLELUIA   John 2:1

℟. Alleluia, alleluia.

There was a wedding at Cana in Galilee,
and the mother of Jesus was there.

℟. Alleluia, alleluia.

GOSPEL

The mother of Jesus was there. And his disciples believed in him.

✠ A reading from the holy gospel according to John   2:1-11

There was a wedding in Cana in Galilee,
and the mother of Jesus was there.
Jesus and his disciples were also invited to the wedding.
When the wine ran short,
    the mother of Jesus said to him,
    "They have no wine."
And Jesus said to her,
    "Woman, how does your concern affect me?
My hour has not yet come."
His mother said to the servers,
    "Do whatever he tells you."
Now there were six stone water jars there for Jewish cere-
        monial washings,
    each holding twenty to thirty gallons.
Jesus told the servers,
    "Fill the jars with water."
So they filled them to the brim.

Then Jesus told them,
> "Draw some out now and take it to the headwaiter."
So they took it.
And when the headwaiter tasted the water that had become
> wine,
>> without knowing where it came from
>> (although the servers who had drawn the water knew),
>> the headwaiter called the bridegroom and said to him,
>> "Everyone serves good wine first,
>> and then when people have drunk freely, an inferior
>>> one;
>> but you have kept the good wine until now."
Jesus did this as the beginning of his signs in Cana in
> Galilee
>> and so revealed his glory,
>> and his disciples began to believe in him.

> The gospel of the Lord.

41. THE BLESSED VIRGIN MARY, MOTHER OF CONSOLATION

FIRST READING

A   The Spirit of the Lord sent me to comfort the brokenhearted.

A reading from the book of the prophet Isaiah   61:1-3, 10-11

The spirit of the Lord GOD is upon me,
    because the LORD has anointed me;
he has sent me to bring glad tidings to the lowly,
    to heal the brokenhearted,
to proclaim liberty to the captives
    and release to the prisoners,
to announce a year of favor from the LORD
    and a day of vindication by our God,
    to comfort all who mourn;
to place on those who mourn in Zion
    a diadem instead of ashes,
to give them oil of gladness in place of mourning,
    a glorious mantle instead of a listless spirit.
They will be called oaks of justice,
    planted by the Lord to show his glory.

I rejoice heartily in the LORD,
    in my God is the joy of my soul;
for he has clothed me with a robe of salvation,
    and wrapped me in a mantle of justice,
like a bridegroom adorned with a diadem,
    like a bride bedecked with her jewels.
As the earth brings forth its plants,
    and a garden makes its growth spring up,
so will the Lord GOD make justice and praise
    spring up before all the nations.

                            The word of the Lord.

B God comforts us that we might comfort others in their sorrows.

A reading from the second letter of Paul to the Corinthians
1:3-7

Brothers and sisters:
Blessed be the God and Father of our Lord Jesus Christ,
the Father of compassion and the God of all encouragement,
who encourages us in our every affliction,
so that we may be able to encourage
those who are in any affliction
with the encouragement with which we ourselves are
encouraged by God.
For as Christ's sufferings overflow to us,
so through Christ does our encouragement also overflow.
If we are afflicted,
it is for your encouragement and salvation;
if we are encouraged,
it is for your encouragement,
which enables you to endure the same sufferings that
we suffer.
Our hope for you is firm,
for we know that as you share in the sufferings,
you also share in the encouragement.

The word of the Lord.

RESPONSORIAL PSALM
Isaiah 12:1, 2-3, 4bcd, 5-6

℟. (3) You will draw water joyfully from the springs of
salvation.

I give thanks, O LORD;
though you have been angry with me,
your anger has abated, and you have consoled me.

℟. You will draw water joyfully from the springs of salvation.

God indeed is my savior;
I am confident and unafraid.
My strength and my courage is the LORD,
and he has been my savior.
With joy you will draw water
at the fountain of salvation.

℟. You will draw water joyfully from the springs of salvation.

Give thanks to the LORD, acclaim his name;
among the nations make known his deeds,
proclaim how exalted is his name.

℟. You will draw water joyfully from the springs of salvation.

Sing praise to the LORD for his glorious achievement;
let this be known throughout all the earth.
Shout with exultation, O city of Zion,
for great in your midst
is the Holy One of Israel!

℟. You will draw water joyfully from the springs of salvation.

ALLELUIA   Matthew 5:5

℟. Alleluia, alleluia.

Blessed are those who mourn,
for they shall be comforted.

℟. Alleluia, alleluia.

GOSPEL

A   Blessed are those who mourn, for they shall be comforted.

✠ A reading from the holy gospel according to Matthew

5:1-12

When Jesus saw the crowds, he went up the mountain, and after he had sat down, his disciples came to him. Jesus began to teach them, saying:
   "Blessed are the poor in spirit,
      for theirs is the kingdom of heaven.
   Blessed are they who mourn,
      for they will be comforted.
   Blessed are the meek,
      for they will inherit the land.
   Blessed are they who hunger and thirst for righteousness,
      for they will be satisfied.
   Blessed are the merciful,
      for they will be shown mercy.
   Blessed are the clean of heart,
      for they will see God.
   Blessed are the peacemakers,
      for they will be called children of God.
   Blessed are they who are persecuted for the sake of righteousness,
      for theirs is the kingdom of heaven.
Blessed are you when they insult you and persecute you
      and utter every kind of evil against you falsely because
         of me.
Rejoice and be glad,
      for your reward will be great in heaven.
Thus they persecuted the prophets who were before you."

The gospel of the Lord.

B

I shall ask the Father, and the Father will give you another Advocate to be with you for ever.

✠ A reading from the holy gospel according to John

14:15-21, 25-27

Jesus said to his disciples:
   "If you love me, you will keep my commandments.
And I will ask the Father,
      and he will give you another Advocate to be with you
         always,
      the Spirit of truth, whom the world cannot accept,
      because it neither sees nor knows it.
But you know the Spirit, because it remains with you,
      and will be in you.
I will not leave you orphans;
      I will come to you.
In a little while the world will no longer see me,
      but you will see me, because I live and you will live.
On that day you will realize that I am in my Father
      and you are in me and I in you.
Those who have my commandments and observe them
      are the ones who love me.
And those who love me will be loved by my Father,
      and I will love them and reveal myself to them.

"I have told you this while I am with you.
The Advocate, the holy Spirit—
      whom the Father will send in my name—
      will teach you everything
      and remind you of all that I told you.
Peace I leave with you; my peace I give to you.
Not as the world gives do I give peace to you.
Do not let your hearts be troubled or afraid."

The gospel of the Lord.

42. THE BLESSED VIRGIN MARY, HELP OF CHRISTIANS

FIRST READING

A   A great sign appeared in the sky.

A reading from the book of Revelation   12:1-3, 7-12ab, 17

A great sign appeared in the sky,
    a woman clothed with the sun,
    with the moon under her feet,
    and on her head a crown of twelve stars.
She was with child
    and wailed aloud in pain as she labored to give birth.
Then another sign appeared in the sky;
    it was a huge red dragon,
    with seven heads and ten horns,
    and on its heads were seven diadems.

War broke out in heaven;
    Michael and his angels battled against the dragon.
The dragon and its angels fought back,
    but they did not prevail
    and there was no longer any place for them in heaven.
The huge dragon, the ancient serpent,
    who is called the Devil and Satan,
    who deceived the whole world,
    was thrown down to earth,
    and its angels were thrown down with it.

Then I, John, heard a loud voice in heaven say:
    "Now have salvation and power come,
      and the kingdom of our God
      and the authority of his Anointed.
For the accuser of our brothers and sisters is cast out,
      who accuses them before our God day and night.
They conquered him by the blood of the Lamb
      and by the word of their testimony;
      love for life did not deter them from death.

Therefore, rejoice, you heavens,
  and you who dwell in them."

Then the dragon became angry with the woman
  and went off to wage war against the rest of her off-
      spring,
  those who keep God's commandments and bear witness
      to Jesus.

The word of the Lord.

B   I will put enmity between you and the woman.

A reading from the book of Genesis   3:1-6, 13-15

Now the serpent was the most cunning of all the animals
  that the LORD God had made.
The serpent asked the woman,
  "Did God really tell you not to eat
  from any of the trees in the garden?"
The woman answered the serpent:
  "We may eat of the fruit of the trees in the garden;
  it is only about the fruit of the tree
  in the middle of the garden that God said,
  'You shall not eat it or even touch it, lest you die.' "
But the serpent said to the woman:
  "You certainly will not die!
No, God knows well that the moment you eat of it
  your eyes will be opened and you will be like gods
  who know what is good and what is evil."
The woman saw that the tree was good for food,
  pleasing to the eyes, and desirable for gaining wisdom.
So the woman took some of its fruit and ate it;
  and she also gave some to her husband, who was with
      her,
  and he ate it.

The LORD God then asked the woman,
  "Why did you do such a thing?"
The woman answered, "The serpent tricked me into it, so I
      ate it."

Then the LORD God said to the serpent:
"Because you have done this, you shall be banned
   from all the animals
   and from all the wild creatures;
on your belly shall you crawl,
   and dirt shall you eat
   all the days of your life.
I will put enmity between you and the woman,
   and between your offspring and hers;
her offspring will strike at your head,
   while you strike at their heel."

The word of the Lord.

RESPONSORIAL PSALM   Judith 16:13, 14, 15

R̥. (2d) Rejoice and call on the name of the Lord.

A new hymn I will sing to my God.
O LORD, great are you and glorious,
wonderful in power and unsurpassable.

R̥. Rejoice and call on the name of the Lord.

Let your every creature serve you;
for you spoke, and they were made,
you sent forth your spirit, and they were created;
no one can resist your word.

R̥. Rejoice and call on the name of the Lord.

The mountains to their bases, and the seas, are shaken;
the rocks, like wax, melt before your glance.
But to those who fear you,
you are very merciful.

R̥. Rejoice and call on the name of the Lord.

ALLELUIA   See Luke 1:45

R̥. Alleluia, alleluia.

Blessed are you, O Virgin Mary, for firmly believing
that the promises of the Lord would be fulfilled.

R̥. Alleluia, alleluia.

GOSPEL

This was the first of Jesus' signs.

✠ A reading from the holy gospel according to John   2:1-11

There was a wedding in Cana in Galilee,
    and the mother of Jesus was there.
Jesus and his disciples were also invited to the wedding.
When the wine ran short,
    the mother of Jesus said to him,
    "They have no wine."
And Jesus said to her,
    "Woman, how does your concern affect me?
My hour has not yet come."
His mother said to the servers,
    "Do whatever he tells you."
Now there were six stone water jars there for Jewish cere-
        monial washings,
    each holding twenty to thirty gallons.
Jesus told the servers,
    "Fill the jars with water."
So they filled them to the brim.
Then Jesus told them,
    "Draw some out now and take it to the headwaiter."
So they took it.
And when the headwaiter tasted the water that had become
        wine,
    without knowing where it came from
    (although the servers who had drawn the water knew),
    the headwaiter called the bridegroom and said to him,
    "Everyone serves good wine first,
    and then when people have drunk freely, an inferior
        one;
    but you have kept the good wine until now."
Jesus did this as the beginning of his signs in Cana in
        Galilee
    and so revealed his glory,
    and his disciples began to believe in him.

The gospel of the Lord.

43. OUR LADY OF RANSOM

FIRST READING

The hand of the Lord strengthened me.

A reading from the book of Judith   15:8-10; 16:13-14

The high priest Joakim and the elders of the Israelites,
    who dwelt in Jerusalem,
  came to see for themselves the good things that the
    LORD had done for Israel,
and to meet and congratulate Judith.
When they had visited her, all with one accord blessed her,
    saying:
  "You are the glory of Jerusalem,
    the surpassing joy of Israel;
    you are the splendid boast of our people.
With your own hand you have done all this;
    you have done good to Israel,
    and God is pleased with what you have wrought.
May you be blessed by the LORD Almighty
    forever and ever!"
And all the people answered, "Amen!"

Judith then said:
  "A new hymn I will sing to my God.
    O LORD, great are you and glorious,
    wonderful in power and unsurpassable.
Let your every creature serve you;
    for you spoke, and they were made,
  you sent forth your spirit, and they were created;
    no one can resist your word."

The word of the Lord.

RESPONSORIAL PSALM   Luke 1:46-48a, 48b-49, 50-51, 52-53, 54-55

℟. The Lord had mercy on his people.

**My soul proclaims the greatness of the Lord;
my spirit rejoices in God my savior.
For he has looked upon his handmaid's lowliness;**

℟. The Lord had mercy on his people.

**Behold, from now on will all ages call me blessed.
The Mighty One has done great things for me,
and holy is his name.**

℟. The Lord had mercy on his people.

**The Lord's mercy is from age to age
to those who fear him.
He has shown might with his arm,
dispersed the arrogant of mind and heart.**

℟. The Lord had mercy on his people.

**He has thrown down the rulers from their thrones
but lifted up the lowly.
The hungry he has filled with good things;
the rich he has sent away empty.**

℟. The Lord had mercy on his people.

**The Lord has helped Israel his servant,
remembering his mercy,
according to his promise to our ancestors,
to Abraham and to his descendants for ever.**

℟. The Lord had mercy on his people.

ALLELUIA   See Luke 1:45

℟. Alleluia, alleluia.

**Blessed are you, O Virgin Mary, for firmly believing
that the promises of the Lord would be fulfilled.**

℟. Alleluia, alleluia.

GOSPEL

Woman, this is your son.

✠ A reading from the holy gospel according to John   19:25-27

Standing by the cross of Jesus were his mother
    and his mother's sister, Mary the wife of Clopas,
    and Mary of Magdala.
When Jesus saw his mother and the disciple whom he loved
        standing beside her,
    he said to his mother, "Woman, behold, your son."
Then he said to the disciple,
    "Behold, your mother."
And from that hour the disciple took her into his home.

The gospel of the Lord.

44. THE BLESSED VIRGIN MARY, HEALTH OF THE SICK

He bore our sufferings himself.

A reading from the book of the prophet Isaiah   53:1-5, 7-10

Who would believe what we have heard?
    To whom has the arm of the LORD been revealed?
The servant grew up like a sapling before him,
    like a shoot from the parched earth;
there was in him no stately bearing to make us look at him,
    nor appearance that would attract us to him.
He was spurned and avoided by people,
    a man of suffering, accustomed to infirmity,
one of those from whom people hide their faces,
    spurned, and we held him in no esteem.

Yet it was our infirmities that the servant bore,
    our sufferings that he endured,
while we thought of him as stricken,
    as one smitten by God and afflicted.
But he was pierced for our offenses,
    crushed for our sins,
upon him was the chastisement that makes us whole,
    by his stripes we were healed.
Though he was harshly treated, he submitted
    and opened not his mouth;
like a lamb led to the slaughter
    or a sheep before the shearers,
    he was silent and opened not his mouth.
Oppressed and condemned, he was taken away,
    and who would have thought any more of his destiny?
When he was cut off from the land of the living,
    and smitten for the sin of his people,
a grave was assigned him among the wicked
    and a burial place with evildoers,
though he had done no wrong
    nor spoken any falsehood.

187

But the LORD was pleased
    to crush his servant in infirmity.
If he gives his life as an offering for sin,
    he shall see his descendants in a long life,
    and the will of the LORD shall be accomplished through
        him.

The word of the Lord.

RESPONSORIAL PSALM   Psalm 103:1-2, 3-4, 6-7, 8 and 10

℟. (1a, 3b) My soul, bless the Lord, who heals all your
        ills.

Bless the LORD, my soul;
all my being, bless his holy name!
Bless the LORD, my soul;
do not forget all the gifts of God.

℟. My soul, bless the Lord, who heals all your ills.

Who pardons all your sins,
heals all your ills,
delivers your life from the pit,
surrounds you with love and compassion.

℟. My soul, bless the Lord, who heals all your ills.

The LORD does righteous deeds,
brings justice to all the oppressed.
God's ways were revealed to Moses,
mighty deeds to the people of Israel.

℟. My soul, bless the Lord, who heals all your ills.

Merciful and gracious is the LORD,
slow to anger, abounding in kindness.
God has not dealt with us as our sins merit,
nor requited us as our deeds deserve.

℟. My soul, bless the Lord, who heals all your ills.

ALLELUIA   See Luke 1:45

℟. Alleluia, alleluia.

**Blessed are you, O Virgin Mary, for firmly believing
that the promises of the Lord would be fulfilled.**

℟. Alleluia, alleluia.

GOSPEL

Why should I be honored with a visit from the mother of my Lord?

✠ **A reading from the holy gospel according to Luke**   1:39-56

M ary set out
   and traveled to the hill country in haste
   to a town of Judah,
   where she entered the house of Zechariah
   and greeted Elizabeth.
When Elizabeth heard Mary's greeting,
   the infant leaped in her womb,
   and Elizabeth, filled with the holy Spirit,
   cried out in a loud voice and said,
   "Most blessed are you among women,
   and blessed is the fruit of your womb.
And how does this happen to me,
   that the mother of my Lord should come to me?
For at the moment the sound of your greeting reached my
         ears,
   the infant in my womb leaped for joy.
Blessed are you who believed
   that what was spoken to you by the Lord
   would be fulfilled."

And Mary said:
   "My soul proclaims the greatness of the Lord;
      my spirit rejoices in God my savior.
   For the Lord has looked upon his handmaid's lowliness;
      behold, from now on will all ages call me blessed.
   The Mighty One has done great things for me,
      and holy is his name.

The Lord's mercy is from age to age
    to those who fear him.
The Lord has shown might with his arm,
    dispersed the arrogant of mind and heart.
The Lord has thrown down the rulers from their thrones
    but lifted up the lowly.
The hungry he has filled with good things;
    the rich he has sent away empty.
The Lord has helped Israel his servant,
    remembering his mercy,
according to his promise to our ancestors,
    to Abraham and to his descendants forever."
Mary remained with Elizabeth about three months
and then returned to her home.

                            The gospel of the Lord.

45. THE BLESSED VIRGIN MARY, QUEEN OF PEACE

FIRST READING

The dominion of the Lord is boundless in a peace that has no end.

A reading from the book of the prophet Isaiah 9:1-3, 5-6

The people who walked in darkness
    have seen a great light;
upon those who dwelt in the land of gloom
    a light has shone.
You have brought them abundant joy
    and great rejoicing,
as they rejoice before you as at the harvest,
    as people make merry when dividing spoils.
For the yoke that burdened them,
    the pole on their shoulder,
and the rod of their taskmaster
    you have smashed, as on the day of Midian.
For a child is born to us, a son is given us;
    upon his shoulder dominion rests.
They name him Wonder-Counselor, God-Hero,
    Father-Forever, Prince of Peace.
His dominion is vast
    and forever peaceful,
from David's throne, and over his kingdom,
    which he confirms and sustains
by judgment and justice,
    both now and forever.
The zeal of the LORD of hosts will do this!

                          The word of the Lord.

RESPONSORIAL PSALM   Psalm 85:9ab-10, 11-12, 13-14

℟. (See 9) The Lord speaks of peace to his people.

I will listen for the word of God;
surely the LORD will proclaim peace
to his people, to the faithful,
to those who trust in him.

Near indeed is salvation for the loyal;
prosperity will fill our land.

R⁰. The Lord speaks of peace to his people.

Love and truth will meet;
justice and peace will kiss.
Truth will spring from the earth;
justice will look down from heaven.

R⁰. The Lord speaks of peace to his people.

The LORD will surely grant abundance;
our land will yield its increase.
Prosperity will march before the Lord,
and good fortune will follow behind.

R⁰. The Lord speaks of peace to his people.

ALLELUIA   See Luke 1:28

R⁰. Alleluia, alleluia.

Hail, Mary, full of grace, the Lord is with you;
blessed are you among women.

R⁰. Alleluia, alleluia.

GOSPEL

You will conceive and bear a son.

✠ A reading from the holy gospel according to Luke   1:26-38

The angel Gabriel was sent from God
    to a town of Galilee called Nazareth,
    to a virgin betrothed to a man named Joseph,
    of the house of David,
    and the virgin's name was Mary.
And coming to Mary, the angel said,
    "Hail, favored one! The Lord is with you."
But Mary was greatly troubled at what was said
    and pondered what sort of greeting this might be.
Then the angel said to her,
    "Do not be afraid, Mary,
    for you have found favor with God.

"Behold, you will conceive in your womb and bear a son,
   and you shall name him Jesus.
He will be great and will be called Son of the Most High,
   and the Lord God will give him the throne of David his
      father,
   and he will rule over the house of Jacob forever,
   and of his kingdom there will be no end."
But Mary said to the angel,
   "How can this be,
   since I have no relations with a man?"
And the angel said to her in reply,
   "The holy Spirit will come upon you,
   and the power of the Most High will overshadow you.
Therefore the child to be born
   will be called holy, the Son of God.
And behold, Elizabeth, your relative,
   has also conceived a son in her old age,
   and this is the sixth month for her who was called
      barren;
   for nothing will be impossible for God."
Mary said, "Behold, I am the handmaid of the Lord.
May it be done to me according to your word."
Then the angel departed from her.

The gospel of the Lord.

46. THE BLESSED VIRGIN MARY, GATE OF HEAVEN

FIRST READING

A I saw the new Jerusalem, as beautiful as a bride all dressed for her husband.

A reading from the book of Revelation   21:1-5a

I, John, saw a new heaven and a new earth.
    The former heaven and the former earth had passed
        away,
    and the sea was no more.
I also saw the holy city, a new Jerusalem,
    coming down out of heaven from God,
    prepared as a bride adorned for her husband.
I heard a loud voice from the throne saying,
    "Behold, God's dwelling is with the human race.
God will dwell with them and they will be his people
    and God himself will always be with them as their God.
God will wipe every tear from their eyes,
    and there shall be no more death or mourning, wailing
        or pain,
    for the old order has passed away."

The One who sat on the throne said,
    "Behold, I make all things new."

                                            The word of the Lord.

B Or reading no. I, 2 in the Appendix, page 201.

RESPONSORIAL PSALM   Psalm 122:1-2, 3-4, 8-9

℟. (See 1b) Let us go rejoicing to the house of the Lord.

I rejoiced when they said to me,
"Let us go to the house of the LORD."
And now our feet stand
within your gates, Jerusalem,

        ℟. Let us go rejoicing to the house of the Lord.

Jerusalem—built as a city
walled round about.
Here the tribes come,
the tribes of the LORD,
as it was decreed for Israel,
to give thanks to the name of the LORD.

R̶. Let us go rejoicing to the house of the Lord.

For family and friends I say,
"May peace be yours."
For the house of the LORD, our God, I pray,
"May blessings be yours."

R̶. Let us go rejoicing to the house of the Lord.

ALLELUIA

R̶. Alleluia, alleluia.

The gates of paradise, closed by Eve,
were reopened by you, O Virgin Mary.

R̶. Alleluia, alleluia.

GOSPEL

Look, the bridegroom comes. Go out to meet him.

✠ A reading from the holy gospel according to Matthew

25:1-13

Jesus told his disciples this parable:
"The kingdom of heaven will be like ten virgins
    who took their lamps and went out to meet the bride-
        groom.
Five of them were foolish and five were wise.
The foolish ones, when taking their lamps,
    brought no oil with them,
    but the wise brought flasks of oil with their lamps.
Since the bridegroom was long delayed,
    they all became drowsy and fell asleep.
At midnight, there was a cry,
    'Behold, the bridegroom!
    Come out to meet him!'
Then all those virgins got up and trimmed their lamps.

The foolish ones said to the wise,
   'Give us some of your oil,
   for our lamps are going out.'
But the wise ones replied,
   'No, for there may not be enough for us and you.
Go instead to the merchants and buy some for yourselves.'
While they went off to buy it,
   the bridegroom came
   and those who were ready went into the wedding feast
     with him.
Then the door was locked.
Afterwards the other virgins came and said,
   'Lord, Lord, open the door for us!'
But he said in reply,
   'Amen, I say to you, I do not know you.'
Therefore, stay awake,
   for you know neither the day nor the hour."

The gospel of the Lord.

APPENDIX

This appendix comprises a number of texts (I. Old Testament Readings with Responsorial Psalms; II. New Testament Readings with Responsorial Psalms; III. Gospel Readings with Alleluia Verses and Verses before the Gospel) taken either from the *Lectionary for Mass* or from the propers of the *Collection of Masses of the Blessed Virgin Mary: Lectionary*. In accord with what has been said in the General Introduction of this volume, no. 4c, the celebrant, with due regard for the mystery being celebrated and for the liturgical season, may use these texts in place of those provided in any particular Mass formulary.

I. OLD TESTAMENT READINGS WITH RESPONSORIAL PSALMS

1. FIRST READING

You have not withheld your only son.

A reading from the book of Genesis   22:1-2, 9-13, 15-18

God put Abraham to the test.
He called to him, "Abraham!"
"Here I am," Abraham replied.
Then God said: "Take your son Isaac, your only one, whom
     you love,
   and go to the land of Moriah.
There you shall offer Isaac up as a holocaust
   on a height that I will point out to you."

When Abraham and Isaac came to the place of which God
     had told him,
   Abraham built an altar there and arranged the wood on
     it.
Next he tied up his son Isaac,
   and put him on top of the wood on the altar.
Then Abraham reached out and took the knife to slaughter
     his son.
But the LORD's messenger called to him from heaven,
     "Abraham, Abraham!"
"Yes, Lord," Abraham answered.
"Do not lay your hand on the boy," said the messenger.
"Do not do the least thing to him.
I know now how devoted you are to God,
   since you did not withhold from me your own beloved
     son."
As Abraham looked about,
   he spied a ram caught by its horns in a thicket.
So he went and took the ram
   and offered it up as a holocaust in place of his son.

Again the LORD's messenger called to Abraham from
    heaven and said:
"I swear by myself, declares the LORD,
that because you acted as you did
in not withholding from me your beloved son,
I will bless you abundantly
and make your descendants as countless
as the stars of the sky and the sands of the seashore;
your descendants shall take possession
of the gates of their enemies,
and in your descendants all the nations of the earth shall
    find blessing—
all this because you obeyed my command."

The word of the Lord.

RESPONSORIAL PSALM   Psalm 16:5 and 8, 9-10, 11

℟. (1) Keep me safe, O God; you are my hope.

LORD, my allotted portion and my cup,
you have made my destiny secure.
I keep the LORD always before me;
with the Lord at my right, I shall never be shaken.

℟. Keep me safe, O God; you are my hope.

Therefore my heart is glad, my soul rejoices;
my body also dwells secure,
for you will not abandon me to Sheol,
nor let your faithful servant see the pit.

℟. Keep me safe, O God; you are my hope.

You will show me the path to life,
abounding joy in your presence,
the delights at your right hand forever.

℟. Keep me safe, O God; you are my hope.

2. FIRST READING

This is nothing else but the house of God and the gate of heaven.

A reading from the book of Genesis   28:10-17

Jacob departed from Beer-sheba and proceeded toward Haran.
When he came upon a certain shrine, as the sun had already set,
  he stopped there for the night.
Taking one of the stones at the shrine, Jacob put it under his head
  and lay down to sleep at that spot.
Then he had a dream: a stairway rested on the ground,
  with its top reaching to the heavens;
  and God's messengers were going up and down on it.
And there was the LORD standing beside him and saying:
  "I, the LORD, am the God of your forefather Abraham
  and the God of Isaac;
  the land on which you are lying
  I will give to you and your descendants.
These shall be as plentiful as the dust of the earth,
  and through them you shall spread out east and west,
    north and south.
In you and your descendants
  all the nations of the earth shall find blessing.
Know that I am with you;
  I will protect you wherever you go,
  and bring you back to this land.
I will never leave you until I have done what I promised you."

When Jacob awoke from his sleep, he exclaimed,
  "Truly, the LORD is in this spot, although I did not know it!"
In solemn wonder he cried out: "How awesome is this shrine!
This is nothing else but an abode of God,
  and that is the gateway to heaven!"

The word of the Lord.

RESPONSORIAL PSALM   Psalm 24:1-2, 3-4ab, 5-6

℞. (2 Chronicles 7:16a) I have chosen and sanctified this
    house.

The earth and what fills it are the Lord's,
the world and those who live there.
For God founded it on the seas,
established it over the rivers.

℞. I have chosen and sanctified this house.

Who may go up the mountain of the Lord?
Who can stand in that holy place?
"The clean of hand and pure of heart,
who are not devoted to idols,
who have not sworn falsely."

℞. I have chosen and sanctified this house.

They will receive blessings from the Lord,
and justice from their saving God.
Such are the people that love the Lord,
that seek the face of the God of Jacob.

℞. I have chosen and sanctified this house.

3. FIRST READING

Your blessed and fruitful virginity is like the bush which Moses saw on Horeb:
though on fire, the bush was not consumed.

A reading from the book of Exodus   3:1-8

M oses was tending the flock of his father-in-law Jethro,
the priest of Midian.
Leading the flock across the desert, he came to Horeb,
    the mountain of God.
There an angel of the LORD appeared to Moses in fire
    flaming out of a bush.
As he looked on, he was surprised to see that the bush,
    though on fire, was not consumed.
So Moses decided,
    "I must go over to look at this remarkable sight,
    and see why the bush is not burned."

When the LORD saw Moses coming over to look at it more
            closely,
    God called out to him from the bush, "Moses! Moses!"
Moses answered, "Here I am."
God said, "Come no nearer!
Remove the sandals from your feet,
    for the place where you stand is holy ground.
I am the God of your ancestor," he continued,
    "the God of Abraham, the God of Isaac, the God of
            Jacob.
Moses hid his face, for he was afraid to look at God.
But the LORD said,
    "I have witnessed the affliction of my people in Egypt
    and have heard their cry of complaint against their slave
            drivers,
    so I know well what they are suffering.
Therefore I have come down to rescue them
    from the hands of the Egyptians
    and lead them out of that land into a good and spacious
            land,
    a land flowing with milk and honey."

                                    The word of the Lord.

RESPONSORIAL PSALM

℟. (8a) The Lord is kind and merciful.

Bless the LORD, my soul;
all my being, bless his holy name!
Bless the LORD, my soul;
do not forget all the gifts of God.

℟. The Lord is kind and merciful.

Who pardons all your sins,
heals all your ills,
delivers your life from the pit,
surrounds you with love and compassion.

℟. The Lord is kind and merciful.

The LORD does righteous deeds,
brings justice to all the oppressed.
God's ways were revealed to Moses,
mighty deeds to the people of Israel.

℟. The Lord is kind and merciful.

Merciful and gracious is the LORD,
slow to anger, abounding in kindness.
As the heavens tower over the earth,
so God's love towers over the faithful.

℟. The Lord is kind and merciful.

4. FIRST READING

A star from Jacob will arise, and a scepter will come forth from Israel.

A reading from the book of Numbers   24:15-17a

Then Balaam gave voice to his oracle:
The utterance of Balaam, son of Beor,
    the utterance of the man whose eye is true,
the utterance of one who hears what God says,
    and knows what the Most High knows,
of one who sees what the Almighty sees,
    enraptured, and with eyes unveiled.
I see him, though not now;
    I behold him, though not near:
A star shall advance from Jacob,
    and a staff shall rise from Israel.

The word of the Lord.

RESPONSORIAL PSALM   Psalm 72:1-2, 7-8, 12-13, 17

℟. (7) Justice shall flourish in his time, and fullness of peace for ever.

O God, give your judgment to the king;
your justice to the son of kings;
that he may govern your people with justice,
your oppressed with right judgment.

℟. Justice shall flourish in his time, and fullness of peace for ever.

That abundance may flourish in his days,
great bounty, till the moon be no more.
May he rule from sea to sea,
from the river to the ends of the earth.

℟. Justice shall flourish in his time, and fullness of peace for ever.

For he rescues the poor when they cry out,
the oppressed who have no one to help.
He shows pity to the needy and the poor
and saves the lives of the poor.

℟. Justice shall flourish in his time, and fullness of peace for ever.

May his name be blessed forever;
as long as the sun, may his name endure.
May the tribes of the earth give blessings with his name;
may all the nations regard him as favored.

℟. Justice shall flourish in his time, and fullness of peace for ever.

5. FIRST READING

The Lord enabled her to conceive and bear a son, whom they named Obed;
he was the father of Jesse, the father of David.

A reading from the book of Ruth
2:1-2, 8-11; 4:13-17

Naomi had a prominent kinsman named Boaz,
of the clan of her husband Elimelech.
Ruth the Moabite said to Naomi,
"Let me go and glean ears of grain in the field
of anyone who will allow me that favor."
Naomi said to her, "Go, my daughter."

Boaz said to Ruth, "Listen, my daughter!
Do not go to glean in anyone else's field;
you are not to leave here.
Stay here with my women servants.
Watch to see which field is to be harvested, and follow them;
I have commanded the young men to do you no harm.
When you are thirsty, you may go and drink from the vessels
the young men have filled."
Casting herself prostrate upon the ground, Ruth said to him,
"Why should I, a foreigner, be favored with your
notice?"
Boaz answered her:
"I have had a complete account of what you have done
for your mother-in-law after your husband's death;
you have left your father and your mother and the land
of your birth,
and have come to a people whom you did not know pre-
viously."

Boaz took Ruth.
When they came together as man and wife,
the LORD enabled her to conceive and she bore a son.
Then the women said to Naomi,
"Blessed is the LORD who has not failed
to provide you today with an heir!

May he become famous in Israel!
He will be your comfort and the support of your old age,
    for his mother is the daughter-in-law who loves you.
She is worth more to you than seven sons!"
Naomi took the child, placed him on her lap, and became his
    nurse.
And the neighbor women gave him his name,
    at the news that a grandson had been born to Naomi.
They called him Obed.
He was the father of Jesse, the father of David.

The word of the Lord.

RESPONSORIAL PSALM   1 Samuel 2:1, 4-5, 6-7, 8abcd

℞. (See 1a) My spirit rejoices in God my Savior.

My heart exults in the LORD,
my horn is exalted in my God.
I have swallowed up my enemies;
I rejoice in my victory.

℞. My spirit rejoices in God my Savior.

The bows of the mighty are broken
while the tottering gird on strength.
The well-fed hire themselves out for bread,
while the hungry batten on spoil.
The barren wife bears seven sons,
while the mother of many languishes.

℞. My spirit rejoices in God my Savior.

The LORD puts to death and gives life;
he casts down to the nether world;
he raises up again.
The LORD make poor and makes rich,
he humbles, he also exalts.

℞. My spirit rejoices in God my Savior.

He raises the needy from the dust;
from the ash heap he lifts up the poor,
To seat them with nobles
and make a glorious throne their heritage.

℞. My spirit rejoices in God my Savior.

6. FIRST READING

A shoot shall come forth from the stump of Jesse.

A reading from the book of the prophet Isaiah   11:1-5, 10

O n that day,
a shoot shall sprout from the stump of Jesse,
    and from his roots a bud shall blossom.
The spirit of the LORD shall rest upon him:
    a spirit of wisdom and of understanding,
a spirit of counsel and of strength,
    a spirit of knowledge and of fear of the LORD,
    and his delight shall be the fear of the LORD.
Not by appearance shall he judge,
    nor by hearsay shall he decide,
but he shall judge the poor with justice,
    and decide aright for the land's afflicted.
He shall strike the ruthless with the rod of his mouth,
    and with the breath of his lips he shall slay the wicked.
Justice shall be the band around his waist,
    and faithfulness a belt upon his hips.

    On that day,
the root of Jesse,
    set up as a signal for the nations,
the Gentiles shall seek out,
    for his dwelling shall be glorious.

The word of the Lord.

RESPONSORIAL PSALM   Psalm 72:1-2, 7-8, 12-13, 17

℟. (7) Justice shall flourish in his time, and fullness of
    peace for ever.

O God, give your judgment to the king;
your justice to the son of kings;
that he may govern your people with justice,
your oppressed with right judgment.

℟. Justice shall flourish in his time, and fullness of
    peace for ever.

That abundance may flourish in his days,
great bounty, till the moon be no more.
May he rule from sea to sea,
from the river to the ends of the earth.

℟. Justice shall flourish in his time, and fullness of
peace for ever.

For he rescues the poor when they cry out,
the oppressed who have no one to help.
He shows pity to the needy and the poor
and saves the lives of the poor.

℟. Justice shall flourish in his time, and fullness of
peace for ever.

May his name be blessed forever;
as long as the sun, may his name endure.
May the tribes of the earth give blessings with his name;
may all the nations regard him as favored.

℟. Justice shall flourish in his time, and fullness of
peace for ever.

7. FIRST READING

This is the time when she who is in labor is to give birth.

A reading from the book of the prophet Micah   5:1-4a

The LORD says:
You, Bethlehem-Ephrathah,
   too small to be among the clans of Judah,
from you shall come forth for me
   one who is to be ruler in Israel;
whose origin is from of old,
   from ancient times.
(Therefore the Lord will give them up, until the time
   when she who is to give birth has borne,
and the rest of his people shall return
   to the children of Israel.)

He shall stand firm and shepherd his flock
   by the strength of the LORD,
   in the majestic name of the LORD, his God;
and they shall remain, for now his greatness
   shall reach to the ends of the earth;
   he shall be peace.

The word of the Lord.

RESPONSORIAL PSALM   Psalm 2:7-8, 10-11ab

℟. (8a) I will give you all the nations for your heritage.

I will proclaim the decree of the LORD,
who said to me, "You are my son;
today I am your father.
Only ask it of me,
and I will make your inheritance the nations,
your possession the ends of the earth."

℟. I will give you all the nations for your heritage.

And now, kings, give heed;
take warning, rulers on earth.
Serve the LORD with fear;
with trembling bow down in homage.

℟. I will give you all the nations for your heritage.

8. FIRST READING

Rejoice greatly, O daughter Zion.

A reading from the prophet Zechariah   9:9-10

**The LORD says:
Rejoice heartily, O daughter Zion,
   shout for joy, O daughter Jerusalem!
See, your king shall come to you;
   a just savior is he,
meek, and riding on an ass,
   on a colt, the foal of an ass.
He shall banish the chariot from Ephraim,
   and the horse from Jerusalem;
the warrior's bow shall be banished,
   and he shall proclaim peace to the nations.
His dominion shall be from sea to sea,
   and from the River to the ends of the earth.**

The word of the Lord.

RESPONSORIAL PSALM   Psalm 72:1-2, 7-8, 12-13, 17

℟. (7) Justice shall flourish in his time, and fullness of peace for ever.

**O God, give your judgment to the king;
your justice to the son of kings;
that he may govern your people with justice,
your oppressed with right judgment.**

℟. Justice shall flourish in his time, and fullness of peace for ever.

**That abundance may flourish in his days,
great bounty, till the moon be no more.
May he rule from sea to sea,
from the river to the ends of the earth.**

℟. Justice shall flourish in his time, and fullness of peace for ever.

For he rescues the poor when they cry out,
the oppressed who have no one to help.
He shows pity to the needy and the poor
and saves the lives of the poor.

℟. Justice shall flourish in his time, and fullness of
peace for ever.

May his name be blessed forever;
as long as the sun, may his name endure.
May the tribes of the earth give blessings with his name;
may all the nations regard him as favored.

℟. Justice shall flourish in his time, and fullness of
peace for ever.

II. NEW TESTAMENT READINGS WITH RESPONSORIAL PSALMS

9. FIRST READING

Where sin increased, there grace abounded all the more.

A reading from the letter of Paul to the Romans   5:12, 17-19

Brothers and sisters:
Through one person sin entered the world,
and through sin, death,
and thus death came to all, inasmuch as all sinned.

For if, by the transgression of one person,
death came to reign through that one,
how much more will those who receive the abundance
of grace
and of the gift of justification
come to reign in life through the one person Jesus
Christ.
In conclusion, just as through one transgression
condemnation came upon all,
so, through one righteous act,
acquittal and life came to all.
For just as through the disobedience of one person
the many were made sinners,
so, through the obedience of the one,
the many will be made righteous.

The word of the Lord.

RESPONSORIAL PSALM   Psalm 40:7-8a, 8b-9, 10, 11

℟. (See 8a and 9a) Here am I, Lord; I come to do your will.

**Sacrifice and offering you do not want;
but ears open to obedience you gave me.
Holocausts and sin-offerings you do not require;
so I said, "Here I am.**

℟. Here am I, Lord; I come to do your will.

Your commands for me are written in the scroll.
To do your will is my delight;
my God, your law is in my heart!"

℞. Here am I, Lord; I come to do your will.

I announced your deed to a great assembly;
I did not restrain my lips;
you, LORD, are my witness.

℞. Here am I, Lord; I come to do your will.

Your deed I did not hide within my heart;
your loyal deliverance I have proclaimed.
I made no secret of your enduring kindness
to a great assembly.

℞. Here am I, Lord; I come to do your will.

10. FIRST READING

Those whom God knew beforehand and predestined.

A reading from the letter of Paul to the Romans   8:28-30

Brothers and sisters:
   We know that all things work for good for those who
      love God,
   who are called according to his purpose.
For those God foreknew he also predestined
   to be conformed to the image of his Son,
   so that the Son might be the firstborn
   among many brothers and sisters.
And those God predestined he also called;
   and those God called he also justified;
   and those God justified he also glorified.

The word of the Lord.

RESPONSORIAL PSALM   Psalm 8:4-5, 6-7a, 7b-9

℟. (2a) O Lord, our God, how wonderful your name in
all the earth.

When I see your heavens, the work of your fingers,
the moon and stars that you set in place—
what are humans that you are mindful of them,
mere mortals that you care for them?

℟. O Lord, our God, how wonderful your name in all the
earth.

Yet you have made them little less than a god,
crowned them with glory and honor.
You have given them rule over the works of your hands,
put all things at their feet.

℟. O Lord, our God, how wonderful your name in all the
earth.

All sheep and oxen,
even the beasts of the field,
the birds of the air, the fish of the sea,
and whatever swims the paths of the seas.

℟. O Lord, our God, how wonderful your name in all the
earth.

11. FIRST READING

Contribute to the needs of God's people and practice hospitality.

A reading from the letter of Paul to the Romans　　12:9-16a

Brothers and sisters:
Let love be sincere;
　hate what is evil,
　hold on to what is good;
　love one another with mutual affection;
　anticipate one another in showing honor.
Do not grow slack in zeal,
　be fervent in spirit,
　serve the Lord.
Rejoice in hope,
　endure in affliction,
　persevere in prayer.
Contribute to the needs of the holy ones,
　exercise hospitality.
Bless those who persecute you,
　bless and do not curse them.
Rejoice with those who rejoice,
　weep with those who weep.
Have the same regard for one another;
　do not be haughty but associate with the lowly.

The word of the Lord.

RESPONSORIAL PSALM　　Psalm 131:1, 2, 3

℟. (See Psalm 57:2c) In you my soul takes refuge, O Lord.

LORD, my heart is not proud;
nor are my eyes haughty;
I do not busy myself with great matters,
with things too sublime for me.

℟. In you my soul takes refuge, O Lord.

**Rather, I have stilled my soul,
hushed it like a weaned child.
Like a weaned child on its mother's lap,
so is my soul within me.**

℟. In you my soul takes refuge, O Lord.

**Israel, hope in the LORD,
now and forever.**

℟. In you my soul takes refuge, O Lord.

12. FIRST READING

As members of Christ all people will be raised, Christ first, and after him all who belong to him.

A reading from the first letter of Paul to the Corinthians

15:20-26

Brothers and sisters:
Christ has been raised from the dead,
    the firstfruits of those who have fallen asleep.
For since death came through a human being,
    the resurrection of the dead came also through a human
        being.
For just as in Adam all die,
    so too in Christ shall all be brought to life,
    but each one in proper order:
    Christ the firstfruits;
    then, at his coming, those who belong to Christ;
    then comes the end,
    when he hands over the kingdom to his God and Father,
    when he has destroyed every sovereignty
    and every authority and power.
For Christ must reign until he has put all his enemies under
        his feet.
The last enemy to be destroyed is death.

The word of the Lord.

RESPONSORIAL PSALM   Psalm 16:5 and 8, 9-10, 11

℞. (1) Keep me safe, O God; you are my hope.

LORD, my allotted portion and my cup,
you have made my destiny secure.
I keep the LORD always before me;
with the Lord at my right, I shall never be shaken.

℞. Keep me safe, O God; you are my hope.

Therefore my heart is glad, my soul rejoices;
my body also dwells secure,
for you will not abandon me to Sheol,
nor let your faithful servant see the pit.

℟. Keep me safe, O God; you are my hope.

You will show me the path to life,
abounding joy in your presence,
the delights at your right hand forever.

℟. Keep me safe, O God; you are my hope.

13. FIRST READING

Victory has been given to us through Jesus Christ.

A reading from the first letter of Paul to the Corinthians

15:54-57

Brothers and sisters:
When that which is corruptible clothes itself with incorruptibility
and that which is mortal clothes itself with immortality,
then the word that is written shall come about:
    "Death is swallowed up in victory.
    Where, O death, is your victory?
    Where, O death, is your sting?"
The sting of death is sin,
    and the power of sin is the law.
But thanks be to God who gives us the victory
    through our Lord Jesus Christ.

The word of the Lord.

RESPONSORIAL PSALM   Psalm 118:14-15, 16-17, 19-21

R. (1a) Give thanks to the Lord, for he is good.

The LORD, my strength and might,
came to me as savior.
The joyful shout of deliverance
is heard in the tents of the victors:
"The LORD's right hand strikes with power.

R. Give thanks to the Lord, for he is good.

The LORD's right hand is raised;
the LORD's right hand strikes with power."
I shall not die but live
and declare the deeds of the LORD.

R. Give thanks to the Lord, for he is good.

Open the gates of victory;
I will enter and thank the LORD.
This is the LORD's own gate,
where the victors enter.
I thank you for you answered me;
you have been my savior.

R. Give thanks to the Lord, for he is good.

14. FIRST READING

Before the world was made, God chose us in Christ.

A reading from the letter of Paul to the Ephesians   1:3-6, 11-12

Blessed be the God and Father of our Lord Jesus Christ,
who has blessed us in Christ
  with every spiritual blessing in the heavens,
  as God chose us in Christ, before the foundation of the
    world,
  to be holy and without blemish before him.
In love God destined us for adoption to himself through
    Jesus Christ,
  in accord with the favor of his will,
  for the praise of the glory of God's grace
  that he granted us in the beloved.

In Christ we were also chosen,
  destined in accord with the purpose of the One
  who accomplishes all things according to the intention
    of his will,
  so that we might exist for the praise of God's glory,
  we who first hoped in Christ.

The word of the Lord.

RESPONSORIAL PSALM   Isaiah 61:10a-d and f, 11; 62:2-3

R̶. (See Ephesians 1:4) God chose us in Christ to be holy
    and without flaw.

I rejoice heartily in the LORD,
in my God is the joy of my soul;
for he has clothed me with a robe of salvation,
and wrapped me in a mantle of justice,
like a bride bedecked with her jewels.

R̶. God chose us in Christ to be holy and without flaw.

As the earth brings forth its plants,
and a garden makes its growth spring up,
so will the Lord GOD make justice and praise
spring up before all the nations.

℟. God chose us in Christ to be holy and without flaw.

Nations shall behold your vindication,
and all kings your glory;
you shall be called by a new name
pronounced by the mouth of the LORD.
You shall be a glorious crown in the hand of the LORD,
a royal diadem held by your God.

℟. God chose us in Christ to be holy and without flaw.

15. FIRST READING

In my flesh I fill up what is lacking in the sufferings of Christ.

A reading from the letter of Paul to the Colossians   1:21-24

Brothers and sisters:
You once were alienated and hostile in mind because of
    evil deeds;
Christ Jesus has now reconciled you
in his fleshly body through his death,
to present you holy, without blemish,
and irreproachable before him,
provided that you persevere in the faith,
firmly grounded, stable,
and not shifting from the hope of the gospel that you
    heard,
which has been preached to every creature under
    heaven,
of which I, Paul, am a minister.

I, Paul, rejoice in my sufferings for your sake,
    and in my flesh I am filling up
    what is lacking in the afflictions of Christ
    on behalf of his body, which is the church.

The word of the Lord.

RESPONSORIAL PSALM   Psalm 116:12-13, 15-16bc, 17-18

℟. (17a) To you, O Lord, I will offer a sacrifice of praise.

How can I repay the LORD
for all the good done for me?
I will raise the cup of salvation
and call on the name of the LORD.

℟. To you, O Lord, I will offer a sacrifice of praise.

Too costly in the eyes of the LORD
is the death of the faithful.
LORD, I am your servant,
your servant, the child of your maidservant;
you have loosed my bonds.

℟. To you, O Lord, I will offer a sacrifice of praise.

**I will offer a sacrifice of thanksgiving
and call on the name of the LORD.
I will pay my vows to the LORD
in the presence of all the people.**

℟. To you, O Lord, I will offer a sacrifice of praise.

16. FIRST READING

He learned obedience and became the source of eternal life.

A reading from the letter to the Hebrews   5:7-9

Brothers and sisters:
In the days when Christ Jesus was in the flesh,
 he offered prayers and supplications with loud cries and
  tears
 to the one who was able to save him from death,
 and he was heard because of his reverence.
Son though he was, Christ Jesus learned obedience from
  what he suffered;
 and when he was made perfect,
 he became the source of eternal salvation for all who
  obey him.

           The word of the Lord.

RESPONSORIAL PSALM   Psalm 31:2-3b, 3c-4, 5-6, 15-16, 20

℟. (17b) Save me, O Lord, in your steadfast love.

In you, LORD, I take refuge;
let me never be put to shame.
In your justice deliver me;
incline your ear to me;
make haste to rescue me!

℟. Save me, O Lord, in your steadfast love.

Be my rock of refuge,
a stronghold to save me.
You are my rock and my fortress;
for your name's sake lead and guide me.

℟. Save me, O Lord, in your steadfast love.

Free me from the net they have set for me,
for you are my refuge.
Into your hands I commend my spirit;
you will redeem me, LORD, faithful God.

℟. Save me, O Lord, in your steadfast love.

But I trust in you, LORD;
I say, "You are my God."
My times are in your hands;
rescue me from my enemies,
from the hands of my pursuers.

℟. Save me, O Lord, in your steadfast love.

How great is your goodness, Lord,
stored up for those who fear you.
You display it for those who trust you,
in the sight of all the people.

℟. Save me, O Lord, in your steadfast love.

III. GOSPEL READINGS WITH ALLELUIA VERSES

17. ALLELUIA VERSE AND VERSE BEFORE THE GOSPEL

> Happy are you, holy Virgin Mary, deserving of all praise;
> from you rose the sun of justice, Christ the Lord.

GOSPEL

What is conceived in her is of the Holy Spirit.

✠ A reading from the holy gospel according to Matthew

1:18-23

This is how the birth of Jesus Christ came about.
When his mother Mary was betrothed to Joseph,
but before they lived together,
she was found with child through the holy Spirit.
Joseph her husband, since he was a righteous man,
yet unwilling to expose her to shame,
decided to divorce her quietly.
Such was Joseph's intention when, behold,
the angel of the Lord appeared to him in a dream and said,
"Joseph, son of David,
do not be afraid to take Mary your wife into your home.
For it is through the holy Spirit
that this child has been conceived in her.
Mary will bear a son and you are to name him Jesus,
because he will save his people from their sins."
All this took place to fulfill
what the Lord had said through the prophet:
"Behold, the virgin shall be with child and bear a son,
and they shall name him Emmanuel,"
which means "God is with us."

The gospel of the Lord.

18. ALLELUIA VERSE AND VERSE BEFORE THE GOSPEL

Hail, O Virgin, Jesse's shoot:
from you rose the sun of justice, Christ the Lord,
the power and wisdom of the Father.

GOSPEL

Is not his mother called Mary?

✠ A reading from the holy gospel according to Matthew

13:54-58

Jesus came to his native place and taught the people in
their synagogue.
They were astonished and said,
    "Where did this man get such wisdom and mighty
        deeds?
Is he not the carpenter's son?
Is not his mother named Mary
    and his brothers James, Joseph, Simon, and Judas?
Are not his sisters all with us?
Where did this man get all this?"
And the people took offense at Jesus.
But Jesus said to them,
    "A prophet is not without honor except in his native
        place
    and in his own house."
And he did not work many mighty deeds there
    because of their lack of faith.

The gospel of the Lord.

19. ALLELUIA VERSE AND VERSE BEFORE THE GOSPEL   See John 8:31

**If you stay in my word you will indeed be my disciples,
and you will know the truth, says the Lord.**

GOSPEL

Whoever has done the will of God is my brother, my sister, and my mother.

✠ **A reading from the holy gospel according to Mark**   3:31-35

The mother of Jesus and his brothers arrived at the house.
Standing outside, they sent word to Jesus and called
him.
A crowd seated around Jesus told him,
"Your mother and your brothers and your sisters
are outside asking for you."
But Jesus said to them in reply,
"Who are my mother and my brothers and my sisters?"
And looking around at those seated in the circle Jesus said,
"Here are my mother and my brothers and my sisters.
For whoever does the will of God
is my brother and sister and mother."

The gospel of the Lord.

20. ALLELUIA VERSE AND VERSE BEFORE THE GOSPEL

> Hail, O Virgin, Jesse's shoot:
> from you rose the sun of justice, Christ the Lord,
> the power and wisdom of the Father.

GOSPEL

Is he not the carpenter, the son of Mary?

✠ **A reading from the holy gospel according to Mark**   6:1-6

Jesus came to his native place, accompanied by his
    disciples.
When the sabbath came Jesus began to teach in the
    synagogue,
    and many who heard him were astonished.
They said, "Where did this man get all this?
What kind of wisdom has been given him?
What mighty deeds are wrought by his hands!
Is he not the carpenter, the son of Mary,
    and the brother of James and Joses and Judas and
        Simon?
And are not his sisters here with us?"
And they took offense at him.
Jesus said to them,
    "A prophet is not without honor except in his native
        place
    and among his own kin and in his own house."
So Jesus was not able to perform any mighty deed there,
    apart from curing a few sick people by laying his hands
        on them.
Jesus was amazed at their lack of faith.
He went around to the villages in the vicinity teaching.

The gospel of the Lord.

21. ALLELUIA VERSE AND VERSE BEFORE THE GOSPEL   See John 14:16

> I shall ask the Father,
> and the Father shall give you another Advocate
> to be with you for ever.

GOSPEL

Stay in the city, until you are clothed with power from on high.

✠ A reading from the holy gospel according to Luke   24:44-53

Jesus said to the eleven and those with him:
> "These are my words that I spoke to you while I was still
>   with you,
> that everything written about me in the law of Moses
> and in the prophets and psalms must be fulfilled."
Then he opened their minds to understand the scriptures.
And Jesus said to them,
> "Thus it is written that the Messiah would suffer
> and rise from the dead on the third day
> and that repentance, for the forgiveness of sins,
> would be preached in his name
> to all the nations, beginning from Jerusalem.
You are witnesses of these things.
And behold I am sending the promise of my Father upon
    you;
> but stay in the city
> until you are clothed with power from on high."

Then Jesus led them out as far as Bethany,
> raised his hands, and blessed them.
As he blessed them he parted from them
> and was taken up to heaven.
The disciples did Jesus homage
> and then returned to Jerusalem with great joy,
> and they were continually in the temple praising God.

                              The gospel of the Lord.

INDEXES

INDEX OF READINGS

INDEX OF PSALMS

INDEX OF CANTICLES

INDEX OF ALLELUIA VERSES AND VERSES BEFORE THE GOSPEL

ALPHABETICAL INDEX OF MASSES